SINGER

SEWING REFERENCE LIBRARY®

Sewing with an Overlock

Cy DeCosse Incorporated
Minnetonka, Minnesota

SINGER

SEWING REFERENCE LIBRARY®

Sewing with an Overlock

Contents

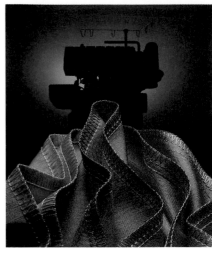

How to Use This Book **7**

Copyright © 1989
Cy DeCosse Incorporated
5900 Green Oak Drive
Minnetonka, Minnesota 55343
1-800-328-3895

Also available from the publisher: *Sewing Essentials, Sewing for the Home, Clothing Care & Repair, Sewing for Style, Sewing Specialty Fabrics, Sewing Activewear, The Perfect Fit, Timesaving Sewing, More Sewing for the Home, Tailoring, Sewing for Children, Sewing Update, 101 Sewing Secrets, Sewing Pants*

That Fit, Quilting by Machine, Decorative Machine Stitching, Creative Sewing Ideas, Sewing Lingerie, Sewing Projects for the Home

Library of Congress
Cataloging-in-Publication Data

Sewing with an Overlock.

p.cm.
(Singer Sewing Reference Library)
Includes index.
1. Machine sewing. 2. Sewing machines.
I. Title: Title: Overlock. II. Series.
TT713.S385   1989   646.2'044—dc19
 88-31343
ISBN 0-86573-247-7
ISBN 0-86573-248-5 (pbk.)

Distributed by: Contemporary Books, Inc.
 Chicago, Illinois

CY DE COSSE INCORPORATED
Chairman: Cy DeCosse
President: James B. Maus
Executive Vice President: William B. Jones

SEWING WITH AN OVERLOCK
Created by: The Editors of Cy DeCosse
 Incorporated, in cooperation with The
 Singer Sewing Company Education
 Department. Singer is a trademark of The
 Singer Company and is used under license.

Project Director & Senior Editor: Rita C. Opseth
Project Manager: Melissa Erickson

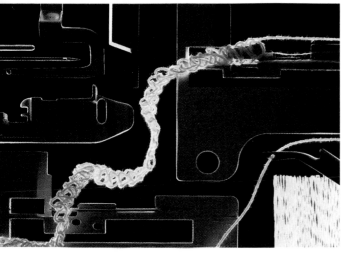

Senior Art Director: Rebecca Gammelgaard
Writers: Karen Drellich, Sue Green
Editors: Janice Cauley, Bernice Maehren
Sample Supervisors: Wendy Fedie,
    Joanne Wawra
Technical Photo Director: Bridget Haugh
Sewing Staff: Phyllis Galbraith, Mary
    Gannon, Bridget Haugh, Joan Coop, Sara
    Holmen, Loy O'Boyle, Carol Olson, Lori
    Ritter, Valerie Ruthardt, Nancy Sundeen,
    Margaret Ulwelling, Barbara Vik,
    John Willcox
Fabric Editor: Marie Castle
Photo Studio Manager: Cathleen Shannon

Photographers: Bobbette Destiche, Rex Irmen,
    Tony Kubat, John Lauenstein, Bill Lindner,
    Mark Macemon, Mette Nielsen, Mark
    Grin, Dan Halsey
Production Manager: Jim Bindas
Assistant Production Managers: Julie
    Churchill, Amelia Merz
Production Staff: Russell Beaver, Holly
    Clements, Sheila DiPaola, Joe Fahey,
    Kevin D. Frakes, Yelena Konrardy, Scott
    Lamoureux, Robert Lynch, Jody Phillips,
    Linda Schloegel, Greg Wallace,
    Nik Wogstad
Consultants: Naomi Baker, John Colbath,
    Zoe Graul, Sue Green, Becky Hanson,

Pam Hastings, Christine Nelson, Nancy
    Rice, Don Ringstrom, Cheryl Wanska
Contributors: Burda Patterns; Chandlers
    Shoes; Clotilde; Coats & Clark; DMC
    Corporation; EZ International; Gingher,
    Inc.; Kwik Sew Pattern Company; Madeira;
    The McCall Pattern Company; Minnetonka
    Mills, Inc.; Pentapco, Inc.; Rowenta, Inc.;
    Simplicity Pattern Company, Inc.; The
    Singer Sewing Company; Swiss-Metrosene,
    Inc.; Tacony Corporation; Vogue/Butterick
    Patterns; YLI Corporation
Color Separations: Spectrum, Inc.
Printing: Ringier America, Inc. (0192)

How to Use This Book

Overlock machines, or sergers, appeared on the home-sewing market about a decade ago. Since then, many different types of machines have been introduced, including machines with three threads, four threads, and five threads.

Look through *Sewing with an Overlock* for inspiration and ideas. The step-by-step photographs will help you learn up-to-date methods for overlocking and how to identify stitch problems. Contrasting thread has been used in many of the photos so the stitches can be seen easily.

Introducing Overlocks

The first section of this book, Introducing Overlocks, shows you the kinds of sewing that can be done on an overlock. You can stitch seams, trim seam allowances, and finish seams all in one step. Learn how an overlock works, and discover the variety of stitches it can make, from standard seams to flatlock to rolled hem.

If you already own an overlock, you may discover new ways to use it. Or, if you are considering buying one, this section may help you decide whether overlock sewing is for you. It offers helpful tips for buying an overlock, using the accessories, selecting just the right thread, and caring for your machine.

You will be introduced to a new vocabulary and even learn how to arrange your sewing room to accommodate the extra machine.

Basic Overlock Techniques

At first, you may be intimidated by this new piece of equipment. The section, Basic Overlock Techniques, helps you through the getting-acquainted process. You can easily learn the quick threading and rethreading techniques and avoid the common threading mistakes that cause stitching problems.

There are special techniques developed for sewing seams and trimming away just the right amount of fabric, for sewing corners and curves, even for

removing stitches the easy way. Practice these methods before sewing a garment to gain confidence and skill.

Adjusting the Stitches

To achieve the best results on each fabric, adjust the stitch length, width, and tension according to the guidelines in the section, Adjusting the Stitches. These pages can serve as a reference as you continue to work with new fabrics and stitches.

This section will help you develop confidence in adjusting the tension dials. Learn what the correct tension looks like for each stitch type and how to adjust your machine to achieve good stitches.

Garment Construction

An overlock makes sewing more efficient than ever before. Discover new methods for stitching collars, hems, cuffs, plackets, waistbands, and waistlines. The section, Garment Construction, includes step-by-step instructions for using your overlock to make pullover tops, blouses, skirts, dresses, and swimwear. Decision making will become easier as you learn when to follow the conventional methods on the pattern guidesheet and when overlock methods might be more suitable.

Find out how to sew special fabrics, such as silkies, sheers, swimwear, and tricot. Learn how easy it is to sew sweaters using the sweater knit fabrics and sweater bodies that overlocks handle so beautifully.

Special Effects

Enjoy creating one-of-a-kind garments with the special effects of decorative stitching. Learn how to achieve custom finishes with your overlock using special threads, such as woolly nylon, rayon, silk, metallic, and topstitching thread, and even ribbon and yarn.

Use the troubleshooting chart when you encounter a stitch problem. With this quick checklist, most problems can be easily solved.

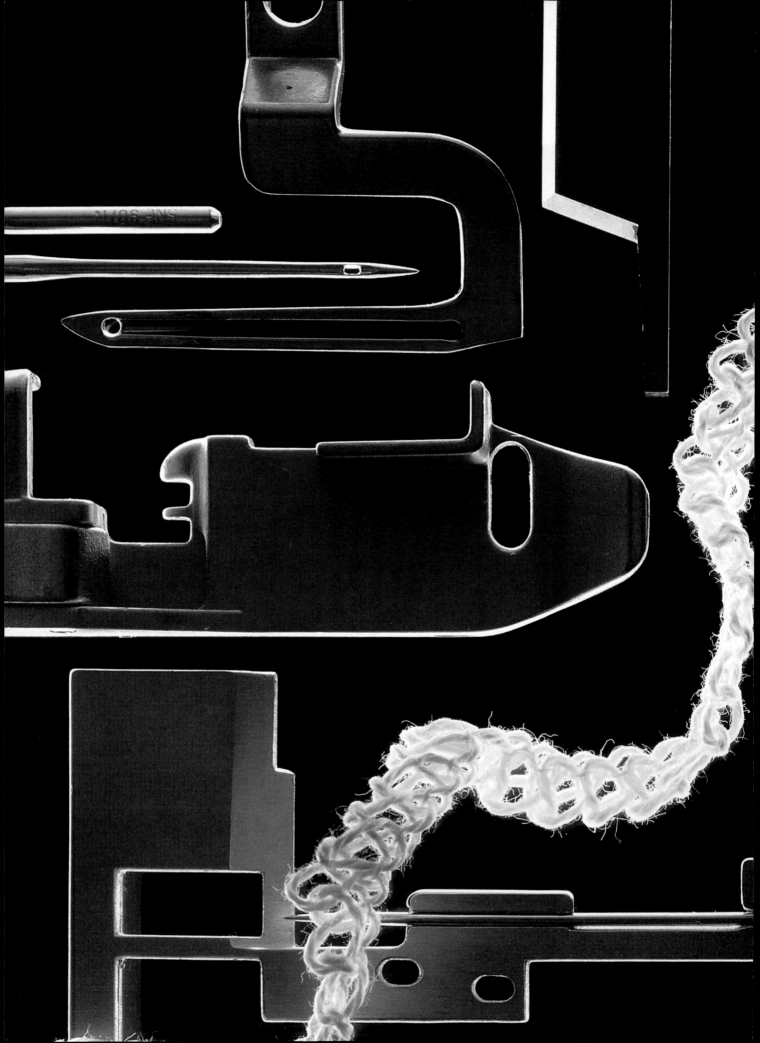

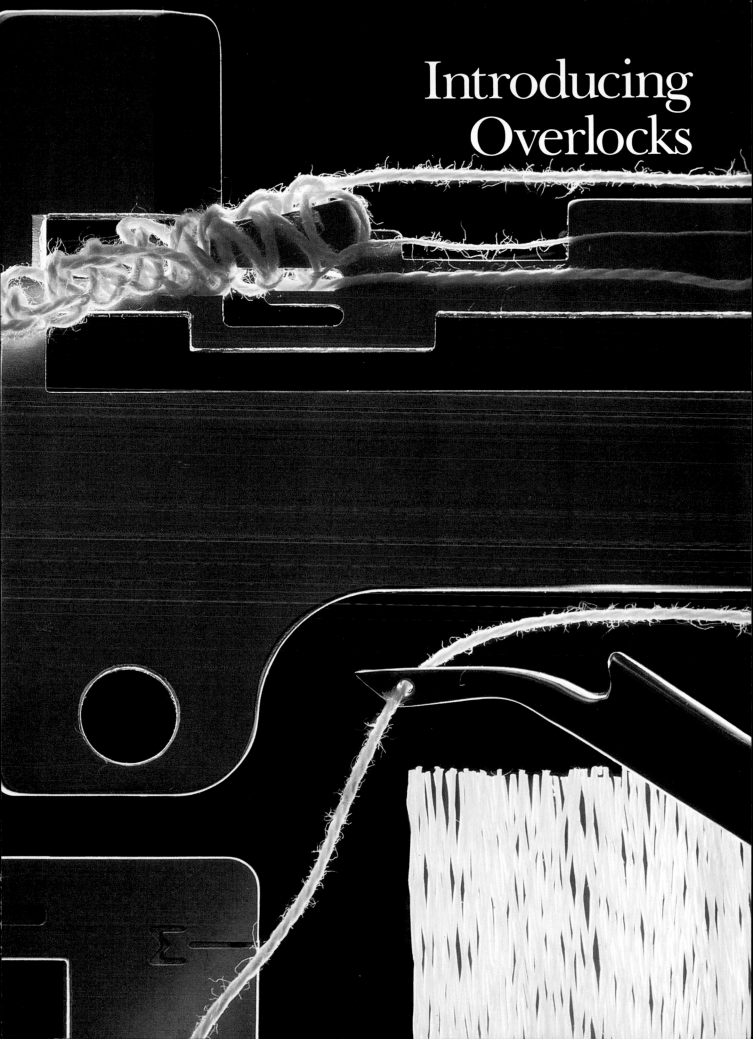

Introducing
Overlocks

Uses for an Overlock

Many busy home sewers want to save time when sewing but are not willing to sacrifice quality. Overlock machines, sometimes called sergers, offer the special stitches of ready-to-wear with faster and easier construction methods.

These machines can sew seams at 1500 stitches per minute, trimming and overcasting the raw edges at the same time for quality seam finishes. Used side by side with your conventional sewing machine, an overlock can add new excitement to home sewing.

Fabrics you previously avoided can be sewn quickly and easily. Overlocks are excellent for stitching seams with built-in stretch for T-shirts and swimwear made from knit fabric. They also excel at sewing all types of woven fabrics, from sheers and silkies to heavy denims.

In addition to the basic stitches for seams and seam finishes, rolled hems and decorative flatlock stitches are also available to add special details to your sewing projects.

Overlocked seam finishes add the look of ready-to-wear to unlined garments.

Pucker-free seams on silky fabrics are fast and easy to sew on an overlock.

Flatlock stitching with decorative thread is used for a special effect.

Rolled hems are narrow, neat edge finishes for rufflcs and hems.

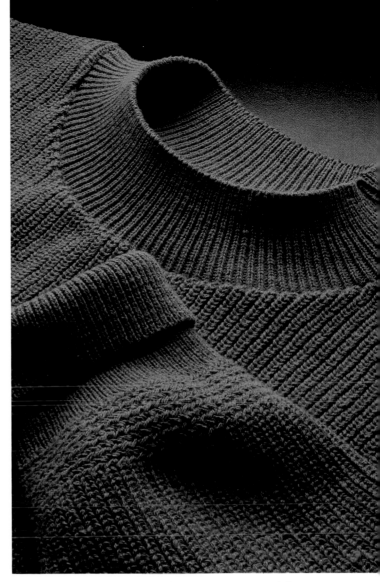

Sweater knit fabrics and ribbings are sewn without fear of the fabric raveling.

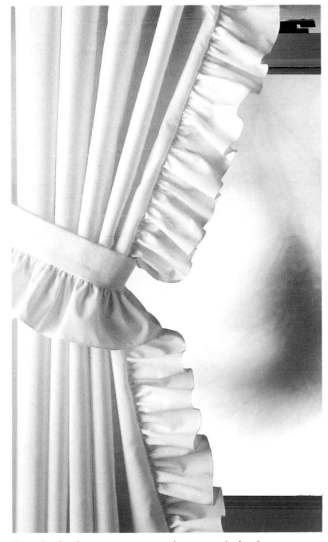

Overlocked seams on curtains are stitched as selvages are trimmed away.

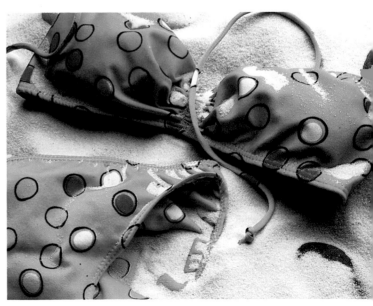

Overlock stitches that stretch are perfect for sewing swimwear from two-way stretch knit fabric.

The Overlock

Many different models of overlocks are available, each offering different types of stitches. Overlocks sew with two, three, four, or five threads. The name of each machine tells which stitches it offers; for example, a 4/3-thread overlock can sew either a 4-thread mock safety stitch or a 3-thread overlock stitch. Each stitch type is unique and serves a special purpose.

An overlock can be identified by type at a glance. Each type has a certain number of needles and loopers, and the shape of the loopers is easily recognized. For a preview of the overlocks available and the stitches they sew, see pages 16 and 17.

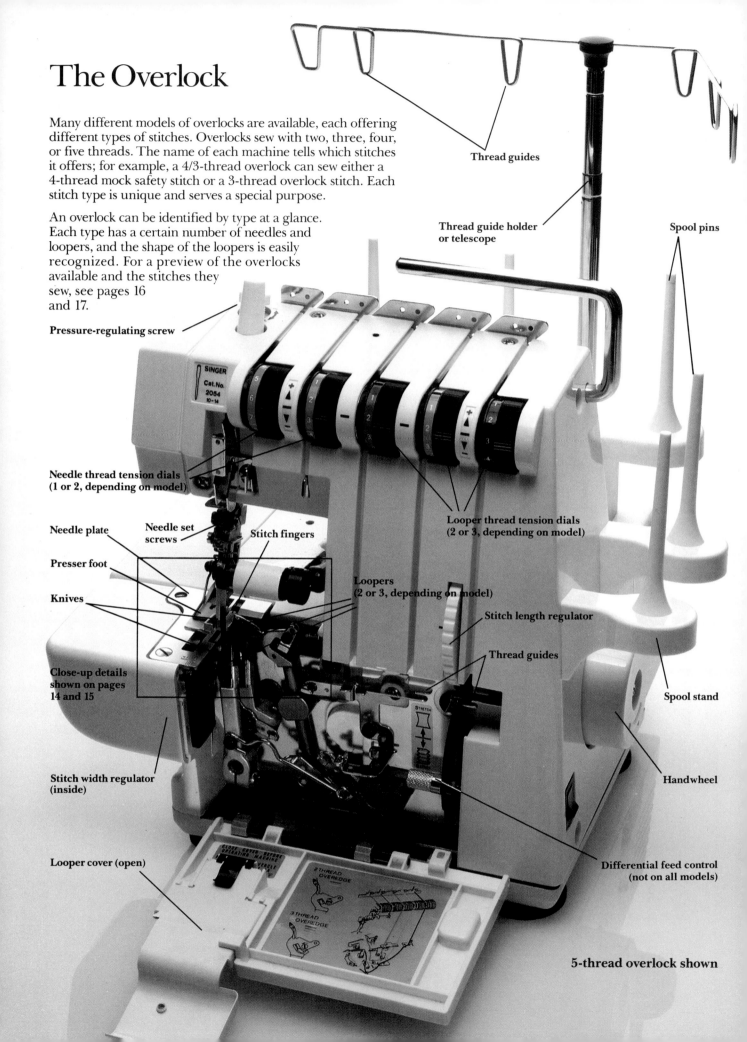

Thread guides

Thread guide holder or telescope

Spool pins

Pressure-regulating screw

Needle thread tension dials (1 or 2, depending on model)

Needle plate

Needle set screws

Stitch fingers

Presser foot

Knives

Looper thread tension dials (2 or 3, depending on model)

Loopers (2 or 3, depending on model)

Stitch length regulator

Thread guides

Close-up details shown on pages 14 and 15

Spool stand

Stitch width regulator (inside)

Handwheel

Looper cover (open)

Differential feed control (not on all models)

5-thread overlock shown

How to Identify Types of Overlocks

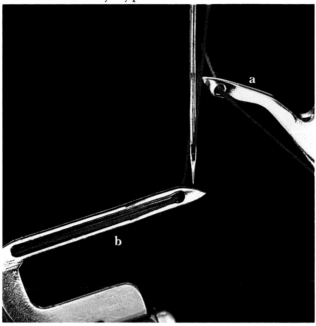

3-thread overlock has one needle and two loopers:
an upper looper (**a**) and a lower looper (**b**). It sews a
3-thread overlock stitch; some models, called
3/2-thread overlocks, convert to sew the 2-thread
overedge stitch.

4/3-thread overlock has two needles and two loopers:
an upper looper (**a**) and a lower looper (**b**). It sews
a 4-thread mock safety stitch similar to the 3-thread
overlock stitch; an extra needle thread secures the
stitches. It sews the 3-thread overlock stitch when
only one needle is used. A 4/3/2-thread overlock also
sews the 2-thread overedge stitch.

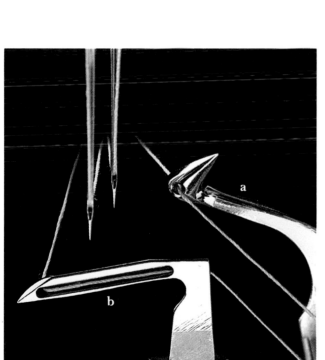

4/2-thread overlock has two needles and two loopers:
an upper looper (**a**) and a chainstitch lower looper (**b**).
It sews a 4-thread safety stitch consisting of a 2-thread
chainstitch and a 2-thread overedge, which are stitched
simultaneously. The chainstitch and the overedge
stitch can each be used separately.

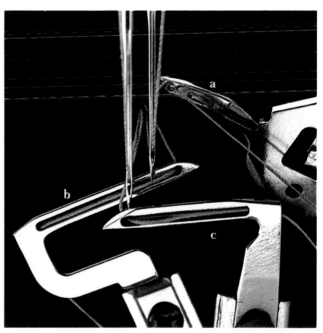

5-thread overlock has two needles and three
loopers: an upper looper (**a**); a lower looper (**b**); and a
chainstitch looper (**c**). It sews a 5-thread safety stitch
consisting of a 2-thread chainstitch and a 3-thread
overlock stitch. Some 5-thread machines also sew a
4-thread safety stitch, a 2-thread overedge stitch, and
a 4-thread or 3-thread mock safety stitch. Each stitch
may be used separately.

Feed system. Feed dogs, needle plate, and presser foot work together to move fabric with even feeding.

Some machines have a differential-feed system to prevent puckered or stretched seams.

How Overlocks Work

Overlocks perform many functions simultaneously to create stitches. As the fabric is fed into the machine, it reaches the feed dogs first. The fabric is moved along until the knives trim the edge. Then the loopers and needles form the stitches on the fabric, and the fabric is fed off the stitch fingers behind the needle.

Cutting system. Seam allowances are trimmed with moveable upper knife **(a)** and stationary lower knife **(b)**; knives work together, like scissors, at the same speed as the needle moves.

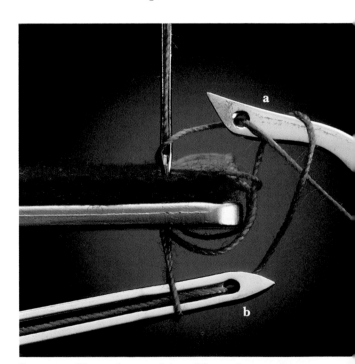

Loopers. Upper looper **(a)** and lower looper **(b)** are used instead of a bobbin to form the stitches. Looper and needle threads lock together to sew seams or seam finishes. Looper threads do not penetrate the fabric.

Stitch fingers. Overlock stitches are formed around one or two stitch fingers, small projections or prongs on the needle plate. Some overlocks also have a stitch finger on the presser foot.

The Stitches & Their Uses

Types of Overlocks	**Types of Stitches**				
	2-Thread Overedge Stitch • lightweight seam finishes • used for wovens	**3-Thread Overlock Stitch** • stretch seams • durable seams or seam finishes • used for knits and wovens	**2-Thread Chainstitch** • stable basting stitch • decorative topstitching • used primarily for wovens	**4-Thread Safety Stitch** • stable seams with lightweight seam finishes • used primarily for wovens	
3-Thread Overlock	on some models				
4/2-Thread Overlock					
4/3-Thread Overlock	on some models				
5/4/3/2-Thread Overlock	on some models			on some models	

16

4-Thread Mock Safety Stitch	Wrapped Overedge Stitch	5-Thread Safety Stitch	Flatlock Stitch	Rolled Hem Stitch
• durable stretch seams • used for knits and wovens	• decorative stitching for edges • used for knits and wovens	• stable seams with durable seam finishes • used primarily for wovens	• flat, nonbulky stretch seams • decorative stitching • used primarily for knits	• narrow hems and seams • decorative stitching • used for knits and wovens

on some models

17

Buying an Overlock

When shopping for an overlock, or serger, keep in mind the same basic questions you would ask if purchasing a conventional sewing machine. Tell the dealer what type of sewing you plan to do, and which fabrics you usually choose. Go shopping with scraps from recent projects you have sewn and samples of fabrics you want to sew. Test the overlock on these scraps and note how the machine handles these fabrics.

Your satisfaction with your overlock will depend, to a great extent, on the dealer you buy from. It is important to purchase a serger from a dealer you trust and like, since you are also buying the service and experience of that dealer. Overlock methods are different from conventional sewing methods, and as a new owner you may feel more comfortable if someone is willing to guide you through the learning process. Find out if lessons are included in the purchase price, and who does the repair service.

There are many features available on sergers. Compare features from model to model to be sure that the machine you purchase will meet your needs. Some features may be more important to you than others, depending on the type of sewing you want to do. For example, the differential feed feature, available on some models, speeds up your sewing if you frequently gather fabric and is helpful for preventing puckered seams on silky fabrics or stretched seams on sweater knits.

By becoming familiar with how overlocks work, you will find it easier to ask related questions and to understand the dealer demonstrations. Before you shop, read about the different types of machines and the stitches they sew (pages 12 to 17).

When overlocks, or sergers, were developed, a new vocabulary was created to define the parts of the machine, the stitches, and overlock sewing techniques. Refer to the chart, below, to become familiar with this new terminology.

The Vocabulary

After stitches. Another name for tail chain.

Balanced stitch. A stitch that is adjusted so threads lock together at the edge of the fabric.

Bight. Another name for stitch width.

Bite. Another name for stitch width.

Chainstitch. A stitch that does not overlock the edge and is sewn on a 4/2-thread or 5-thread machine. Sometimes referred to as safety stitch.

Curling stitch. Another name for rolled hem stitch.

Differential feed. A feature available on some models that prevents puckered or stretched seams and is used to gather fabrics.

Flatlock stitch. A specialty stitch, formed with 2 or 3 threads, that is used for decorative stitching.

Knives. The blades in an overlock trimming or cutting assembly that trim the fabric.

Ladder side of stitch. The horizontal stitch formation on the underside of a flatlock stitch.

Loopers. Parts of a machine that form the stitch.

Merrow. The commercial or industrial stitch that is the same as a narrow or rolled hem.

Mock safety stitch. Commonly, the 4-thread stitch sewn on a 4/3-thread overlock; a 3-thread mock safety stitch is also available.

Overcast stitch. Another name for overedge stitch.

Overedge stitch. A stitch that finishes the edge of the fabric to prevent raveling but is not used for seaming.

Overlock machine. Sewing machine that simultaneously stitches, trims, and finishes seams.

Overlock stitch. A stitch that locks together at the edge of the seam allowance, finishing the edges as well as sewing the seam.

Rolled hem stitch. A stitch that rolls under the edge of the fabric and covers it with thread.

Safety stitch. Another name for chainstitch.

Serger. Another name for an overlock machine.

Stitch finger. The metal prong or prongs on the needle plate or presser foot. Stitches form around the stitch finger and the fabric edge at the same time. Completed stitch is fed off the back of the finger.

Stitch length. The distance in millimeters between the needle penetrations.

Stitch prong. Another name for stitch finger.

Stitch width. The distance in millimeters between the needle thread and the trimmed edge of the fabric.

Tail chain. Stitches, formed over stitch finger, that are locked together and left on the machine after the seam is completed.

Tension dial. The part of the machine that is turned to adjust the tension of each thread.

Tension disc. An internal pressure plate in the tension assembly. Each disc is adjusted by turning the tension dial, creating pressure, or tension, on the thread to regulate stitch formation.

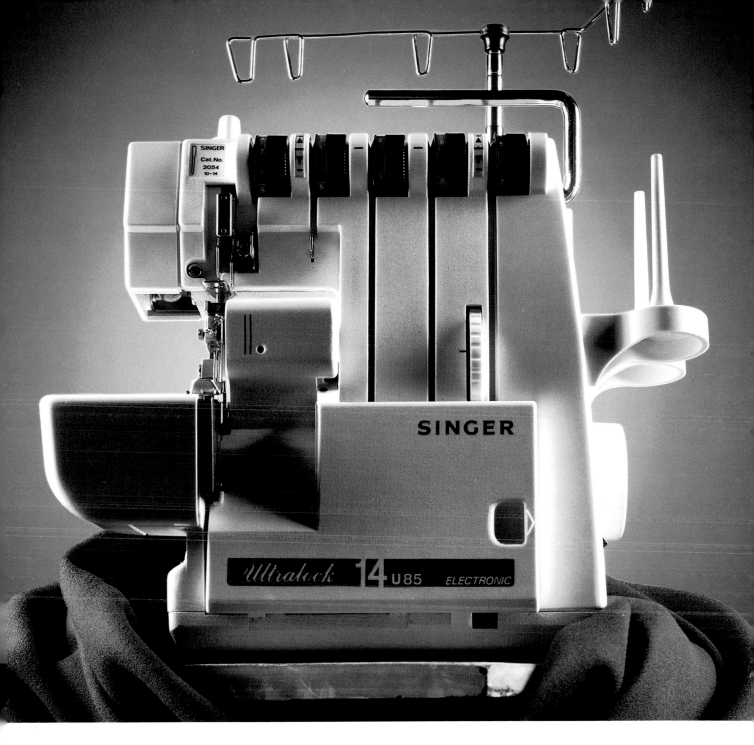

Tips for Shopping

Assemble fabrics of several weights and types you want to sew. Have the dealer demonstrate using these fabrics.

Have the dealer explain the stitches available and adjustments required for changing from one stitch to another.

Have the dealer explain the stitch width and length adjustments; these vary from one model to another.

Have all features, such as differential feed and rolled hem, explained and demonstrated.

Use a striped fabric to practice cutting exactly on a line with the knives; then stitch so the needle runs along a line to see how well you can control the machine.

Have the dealer completely thread the machine. Then thread the machine yourself from start to finish. (The dealer may show you how to thread the machine by tying thread on, but it is still important that you are capable of threading the machine manually).

Ask questions throughout the demonstration to be sure each step is clear in your mind.

Turn each tension dial a little at a time. Check stitching to see how it is affected.

Turn the tension dials at random; then, see how easily you can restore the perfect stitch with dealer's assistance.

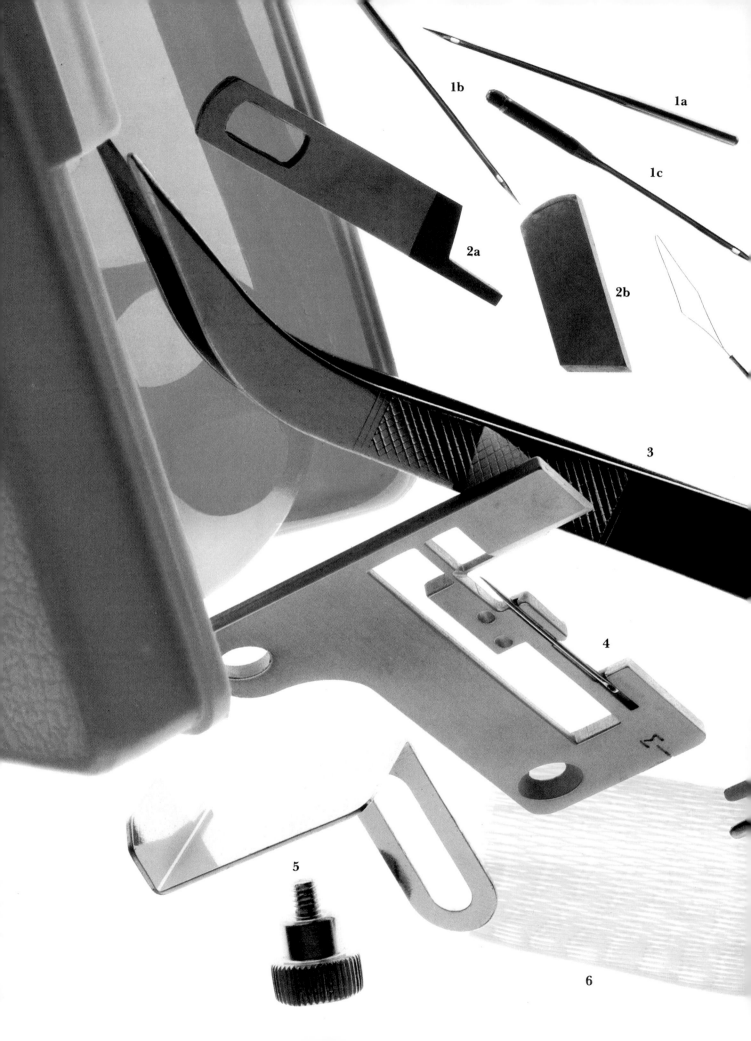

1b

1a

1c

2a

2b

3

4

5

6

Accessories

Every overlock or serger comes with an accessory kit. The instruction manual that comes with the machine describes the use for each tool. The accessories supplied with an overlock will vary, depending on the model. Learning to use them correctly will make sewing time more productive.

Needles vary from one model to another. Industrial needles are available with flat (**1a**) or round (**1b**) shank; conventional sewing machine needles (**1c**) can be used in some overlocks. Check the overlock instruction manual for the correct type of needle to be used in your machine.

Knives trim the excess seam allowances before the seam is stitched. The upper blade (**2a**) is movable and cuts against the stationary lower blade (**2b**) with the same action as scissors.

Tweezers (3) are helpful for threading a serger and are useful in areas with limited space for fingers. Hold the end of the thread with a tweezer while guiding it through the eye of a looper or needle. Tweezers are available in two styles.

Rolled hem plate (4) is used for the rolled hem stitch. Some brands may also require the use of a rolled hem presser foot. These attachments may or may not come with the machine at the time of purchase. Some brands also require extra needle plates with stitch fingers of different sizes to change the stitch width.

Edge guide (5) may be provided for guiding folded fabric evenly when sewing blind hems. Some models have a blind hem foot, similar to a conventional sewing machine blind hem foot.

Nets (6) prevent specialty threads from tangling or slipping off the spools. Use them with rayon, metallic, and parallel-wound monofilament nylon thread.

Spool caps (7) provide even feeding of thread from conventional spools. They are placed directly on the spools. Notch on the rim of the spool should be on the lower end.

Looper threader (8) may be used to thread the lower looper. It is also useful for threading the eye of a needle.

Tape guide (9) is provided for some models. It is used to apply elastic, trims, or ribbons to fabric edges. Some models have a presser foot with a slot that guides elastic or trims; others have a special elastic foot that stretches the elastic while guiding it.

3

9

7

8

Buying Thread

An overlock or serger uses more thread than a conventional sewing machine, so thread companies now offer thread in cones **(1)**, king tubes **(2)**, and compact tubes **(3)**. Tubes and cones have at least 1,000 yards (920 m) of thread, and cones can have as many as 6,000 yards (5720 m).

All-purpose thread may also be used on the serger; it is available on parallel-wound **(4)** or cross-wound **(5)** spools. Parallel-wound spools require the use of a spool cap (page 21) for even feeding. There is a wider color selection in all-purpose thread; use it for mediumweight or heavyweight fabrics when color-matching is critical.

Overlock threads are generally lighter in weight than all-purpose sewing threads. A lightweight thread is generally recommended for serger use. There is more thread in a serged seam and a lighter-weight thread reduces bulk.

Decorative threads, including metallic thread **(6)**, topstitching thread **(7)**, woolly nylon **(8)**, and lightweight ribbons **(9)** and yarns **(10)**, may also be used on a serger (pages 120 and 121).

Sergers will sew with threads of 100% cotton, 100% synthetic, or cotton and synthetic blends. All these thread types work well, although cotton threads can create lint in the tension discs, and synthetics can leave a sticky residue. Although this is

normal, the lint and residue must be cleaned out of the tension discs occasionally. Use the knotted-thread method (page 26) for thorough cleaning.

Determining Thread Quality

Use threads that are fine and evenly twisted with few or no loose fibers. Threads with excess fibers and uneven areas will not produce a perfect stitch. If the stitch quality cannot be improved by machine tension adjustments, change the brand or type of thread you are using. A thread may sew well on one fabric and not on another.

Overlock machines sew at a higher rate of speed than conventional sewing machines and create more stress on the threads. Therefore, threads need to be strong and durable. Test thread for strength; poor-quality thread may break easily in some spots. Use the best quality of thread you can; bargain threads sometimes cause more problems than the savings are worth.

If the thread is wavy when it becomes low on the cone or spool, do not continue to use it on the serger. This wavy thread can cause stitching problems, and the seam may pucker when the garment is laundered. Save this thread for hand sewing.

Using Bobbins on an Overlock

To avoid buying several spools of each color, wind thread on the bobbins of the conventional machine. Use the bobbins on the spool pins of the serger to thread the needles, where the least amount of thread is used, and use the cones to thread the loopers. If a bobbin will not fit over the spool pin, place it in a cup or glass behind the machine. As you stitch, the container will allow a free flow of the thread while the bobbin bounces around.

col. o2

o.150

PES SWISS MADE

1

2

3

5

4

Blending thread colors allows stitches to blend easily with fabric. It is not always necessary to use a thread color that matches the fabric, and you may even blend several shades in the same seam. A supply of serger threads should include colors that blend easily, such as ivory, gray, or rose. Threads in the primary colors of red, yellow, and blue do not blend with many colors of fabric. If you have only one spool of matching thread, use it in the needle at the seamline, and use colors that blend for the other threads.

Organizing the Sewing Room

Sewing room organization is a major contributing factor to successful sewing. Even small spaces can yield comfortable work areas in the home.

For comfortable and productive sewing, both the serger and the conventional sewing machine should be within easy reach and placed so you can move from one machine to the other, without changing chairs. A rolling chair is a good choice; it works best on a clear mat over carpeting or on an uncarpeted floor.

Many manufacturers of sewing room furniture are producing cabinets and tables to accommodate both of these machines.

One design is a corner unit, which places the machines at right angles to each other; another places the machines side by side. There are also fold-up table units to fit either the serger or the conventional sewing machine. These units require a minimum of storage space.

Cone thread racks contribute to an organized sewing room. A selection of basic colors of serger thread should be placed near the sewing area for convenience.

Good lighting is essential. Natural light, although ideal, is not always available. There are many auxiliary lamps available for the home sewer, including lamps that can be clamped onto a table edge and small, detachable lamps designed to attach to the machine.

Sewing Lamps

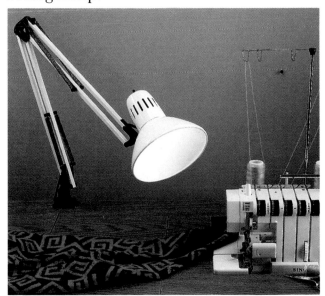

Adjustable arm or gooseneck lamps allow for perfect positioning of the light source.

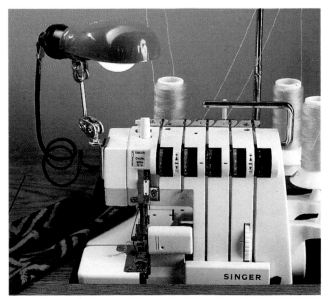

Some lamps may be attached to the machine. They are especially helpful if the machine does not have a built-in light.

Maintenance

Proper maintenance of the machine can prevent costly repairs. A regular routine of cleaning and oiling will ensure many years of trouble-free operation. Overlocks need to be cleaned and oiled more frequently than conventional sewing machines because they operate at high speed and the internal parts rotate more often. Replace needles for good stitch quality, and replace knives to ensure smooth, even trimming, as necessary.

Cleaning & Oiling

Overlock knives create a great deal of lint, which must be cleaned from the machine frequently, using a dry lint brush.

Consult the instruction manual for instructions on oiling your overlock. A pinpoint oiler, left, is especially convenient for reaching all places without dripping.

Use sewing machine oil; oil intended for household use should not be used, because it is too heavy. (If liquid fray preventer is used accidentally instead of sewing machine oil, it will have to be removed by a sewing machine service technician.)

On the average, the machine should be oiled after every eight hours of actual running or "pedal-down" time. A serger should run with a smooth, humming sound; if it does not, it needs oil. Also oil a serger

Tips for Overlock Maintenance

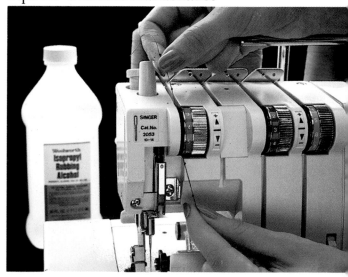

Cleaning tension discs. Tie several knots in a 6" to 10" (15 to 25.5 cm) length of buttonhole twist; soak in rubbing alcohol. Work knotted thread back and forth between tension discs several times to remove lint buildup.

that has been sitting unused for two months, because oil drains to the bottom of the machine.

Replacing Needles

Some overlocks sew with industrial needles; others use the same type of needles as conventional sewing machines. Some industrial needles have a round shank, and others have flat shanks. If you are unsure of the type of needle your overlock uses, consult the instruction manual. Needles are not interchangeable.

Overlock needles wear out quickly, because overlocks sew at a high speed. Needles that are dull, bent, or burred will cause stitching problems. If skipped stitches, uneven stitches, or puckered seams occur, change the needle. If the problem is still not corrected, try a second new needle; occasionally, a new needle is defective. Also change the needle size for different fabric weights, as you do for conventional machines.

Replacing Knives

Knives wear out periodically and require replacement. They should not be sharpened. The instruction manual gives specific information on how to change knives for your model.

Overlocks are designed with a dual-blade cutting system, which uses a stationary lower blade and a movable upper blade. The upper blade is made of a strong carbide steel and does not wear out as quickly as the lower blade, of softer steel. Carbide steel blades are more expensive than softer steel blades.

While softer steel blades do need to be replaced more frequently, it is an asset to have one softer blade if a

pin is accidentally hit. Then, the softer, less-expensive blade is damaged, because it gives, and the carbide blade may not be damaged at all.

During normal use, the lower blade may need to be replaced after three to six months; the upper blade may last from one to five years.

The fiber content of the fabrics you sew affects the performance of the blade. If you frequently sew synthetics, especially polyester, nylon, or spandex, you may need to replace the lower blade as often as every month.

If the trimmed fabric is ragged, check the alignment of the blades. The lower blade may have slipped out of position if there has been a fabric jam, if you hit a pin accidentally, or if the set screw has loosened.

If the knives are correctly aligned and the trimmed fabric is ragged, the lower blade needs replacing. It also needs replacing if trimming causes pulled threads on lightweight fabrics.

If the fabric still does not trim neatly after a new lower blade has been correctly replaced, change the upper blade. The upper blade should also be changed whenever there is noticeable damage to the cutting edge, such as a nick.

The first time you need to replace the upper blade, take it to the dealer, and watch as the blade is correctly installed. It is very important that the upper blade be correctly aligned with the lower blade; if incorrectly positioned, it can cause either jammed fabric or damage to the blades.

Replacing a round-shank needle. Insert new needle as far as it will go, with long groove on needle toward the front. Insert point of another needle into the eye; rotate it until parallel to needle plate for proper alignment. Tighten set screw.

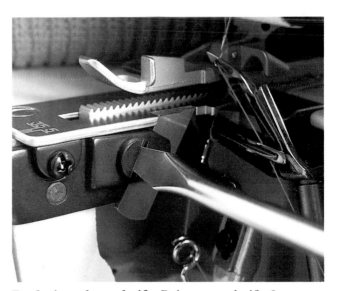

Replacing a lower knife. Raise upper knife. Loosen set screw; remove lower knife. Insert new knife so top of blade is level with needle plate. Tighten set screw. Rotate handwheel several times before sewing on fabric to mesh cutting edges of blades and to remove any uneven areas on new blade.

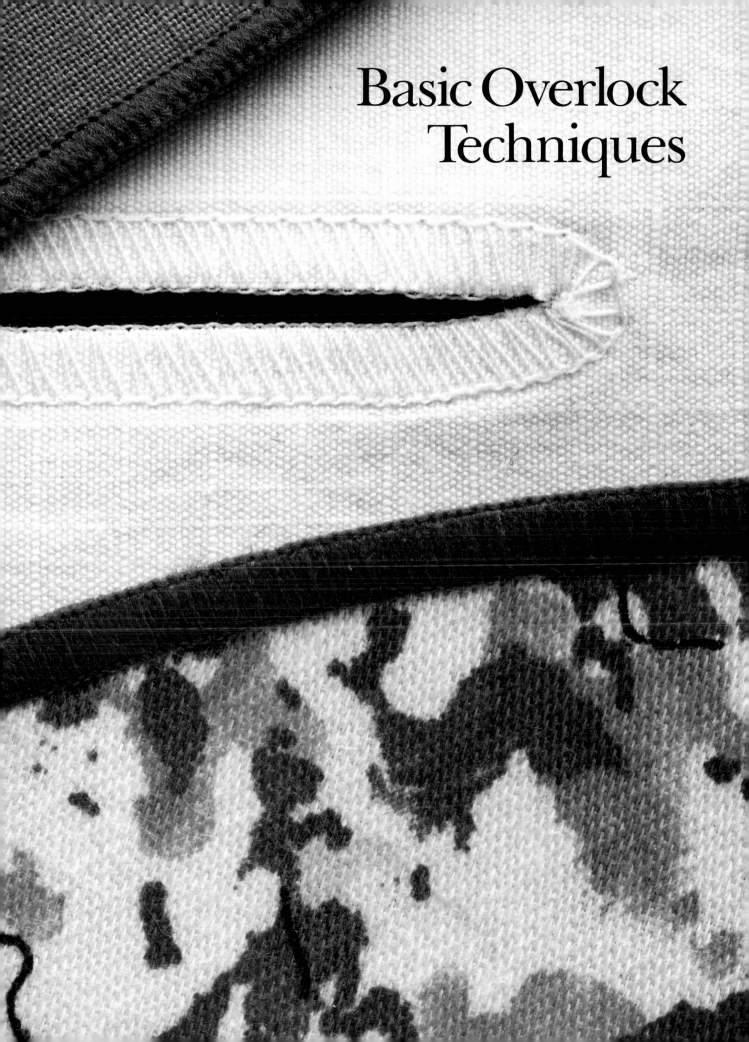

Basic Overlock Techniques

Threading an Overlock

Threading an overlock or serger appears to be complicated at first, but with practice it is not difficult. An easy method for threading an overlock is the tying-on method. Simply cut the old threads and tie on new ones; then pull each new thread through the machine, using the tail of the old thread.

When a thread breaks, or if the machine is run until a spool is empty, it is necessary to thread the serger manually. Carefully place each thread in the proper path, following the threading guide in the instruction manual or on the door of the serger. It is important that the machine be threaded correctly, or it will not stitch correctly. Consult your dealer if you have questions.

Check the threading of the overlock whenever it does not stitch correctly; a thread may not be in all the thread guides, or threads may be tangled. Be sure the thread stand is completely extended and that a thread is not caught around the thread stand, under a spool, or on a thread guide.

Tips for Manual Threading

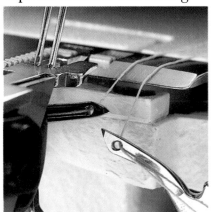

Rotate handwheel until loopers are positioned so they do not cross, before threading lower looper. If lower looper is threaded when it crosses upper looper, threads will tangle, and overlock will not stitch.

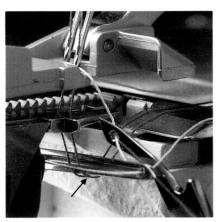

Thread needles last. If needles are threaded before loopers, needle threads (blue) loop under lower looper and become trapped (arrow), and overlock will not stitch unless you draw threads above needle plate, as shown at right.

Draw threads above the needle plate, using tweezers or seam ripper, before stitching if needles are threaded before loopers; this prevents tangling.

How to Thread an Overlock Using the Tying-on Method

1) Clip threads just in front of the needles. (Your machine may have only one needle.)

2) Hold tail chain, and run machine slowly until you have 3" to 4" (7.5 to 10 cm) of straight threads behind the presser foot. (A chain will not form because the needles are not threaded.)

3) Cut threads close to spools on thread stand. Place new threads on stand. Tie new and old threads together. Clip threads 1" (2.5 cm) from knot; if you clip tails close to knot, threads may come untied.

4) Remove threads from each tension dial by pulling above and below dial. Raise presser foot.

5) Pull one tied-on knot through machine, pulling gently on thread end from behind presser foot. If thread does not pull easily, check whether it is caught on thread guide or wrapped around thread stand. Pull other threads through machine, one at a time.

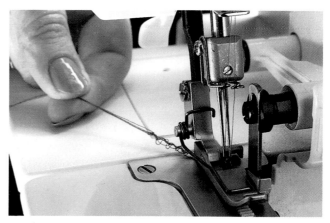

6) Replace threads in tension dials by pulling snugly between tension discs. Thread needles after cutting off knots. Bring all threads under, and slightly to the left of, presser foot. Lower presser foot. Run machine slowly to form tail chain.

Basic Overlock Techniques

The overlock knives trim the fabric approximately ⅝" (1.5 cm) before the needle and loopers form the stitches. When operating an overlock, watch the knives instead of the needle. Sewing mistakes are easy to correct; trimming mistakes are not.

Allow the knives to trim the fabric slightly, even if you are sewing a seam finish, so there will be a neat raw edge for the machine to overedge. A seam allowance that has started to ravel is irregular; if it is not trimmed by the knives, the stitches will be uneven in appearance.

Practice sewing on scraps before sewing garments to become familiar with exactly where the knife blades

are and how they work. You may want to use a striped fabric. Learn to guide the fabric so you trim exactly on one of the stripes. Then become familiar with the needle placement, guiding the striped fabric so you stitch exactly on a stripe.

When seams are serged, the needle stitches on the seamline. (For a machine with two needles, the left needle stitches on the seamline.) When ⅝" (1.5 cm) seam allowances are allowed, stitch so the left needle is ⅝" (1.5 cm) from the edge of the fabric. The knives will automatically trim off the correct amount.

Tips for Guiding Fabric

Mark front of presser foot directly in front of each needle, using permanent marking pen. Guide fabric, positioning seamline at mark. When sewing with two needles, use mark for left needle.

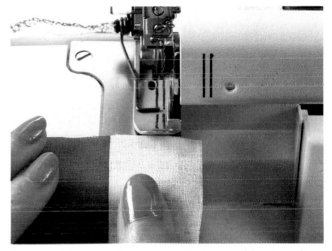

Use markings on door of overlock to guide raw edge of fabric. If machine does not have markings, use topstitching tape or masking tape to mark machine.

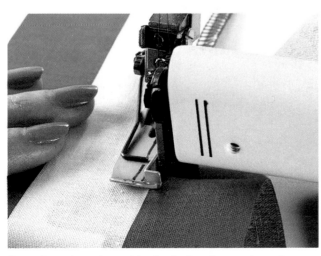

Practice trimming with the knives by sewing along one of the stripes in a striped fabric until you can trim evenly and accurately.

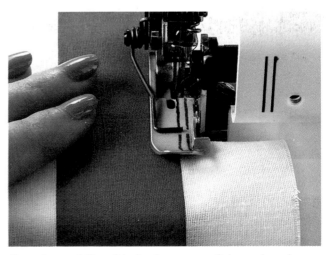

Practice guiding fabric along one of the stripes in a striped fabric, so needle stitches exactly on a stripe.

Basting Seams

Basting seams to check the fit of a garment can be even more important when sewing with an overlock or serger than when sewing with a conventional machine. When seams are sewn on the serger, there are no seam allowances left to be let out.

When sewing with an overlock, use as few pins as possible to reduce the risk of damaging the machine or its knives. If a pin is hit by the knives, one or both knives may need to be replaced, and the timing may need to be serviced professionally. When pins are used, be especially careful to remove each pin as it approaches the knives. For loosely woven or bulky fabrics, use large pins, such as quilting pins; short, fine pins can get lost in these fabrics.

As an alternative to pin-basting, you may want to use a water-soluble glue stick (1) or basting glue (2). Apply water-soluble glue stick to seam allowances, using the edge of the tube to apply dots of glue stick sparingly. Apply water-soluble basting glue to seam allowances in a line or as dots. Glue stick and basting glue do not interfere with trimming, but may cause skipped stitches if too much has been applied.

Basting tapes (3) are also convenient for basting; some, but not all, basting tapes are water-soluble. If basting tape is not water-soluble, place it beyond the 5⁄8" (1.5 cm) seamline so it can be removed after stitching, or at the raw edge so it is completely trimmed away with knives. If basting tape is water-soluble, you may stitch or cut through it.

Tips for Pin-basting Seams

Place pins vertically to the left of the presser foot to eliminate the risk of hitting them with the knives.

Place pins horizontally to secure tucks, pleats, or other details; remove pins as they approach knives.

Sewing Seams

In garment construction, one seam is usually stitched and then intersected by another seam or seam finish. For example, the side seam of a skirt is stitched and then intersected by seams at the waistline and hem. When one seam is intersected by another, the tail chain at the end of the first seam is trimmed away by the second seam. For fragile fabrics or seams that will be stressed, the stitches at the intersecting seams can be reinforced, as shown above. Instructions for this method are on page 36.

Sewing On & Off

When serging seams or seam finishes, you may sometimes need to overlap beginning and ending stitches. This can occur on circular edges, such as a neckline or the lower edge of a skirt, or when you have removed stitches for part of a seam, and the seam needs restitching.

One fast way to begin stitching circular edges is to stitch gradually onto the fabric at an angle; if you want to trim seam or hem allowances, stitch onto the fabric at an angle until you have cut into the edge of fabric as far as desired. Then straighten the fabric and continue stitching and trimming parallel to the edge. To stop sewing, you can simply stitch gradually toward the edge at an angle. Run about 3" (7.5 cm) of tail chain after stitching, as usual. When stitches are overlapped for 1" (2.5 cm), the tail chain may be trimmed close to stitching.

Another method is to clear the stitch fingers and lower the needle into the fabric at the seamline. This method is sometimes preferred because it prevents the gradual looping of threads over the edge of fabric. You may use this method for restitching an area of a seam or for seams and hem finishes that do not require trimming away fabric.

You may want to practice these techniques (shown on pages 36 and 37) on scraps of fabric a few times to gain confidence before sewing garments.

How to Sew a Seam

1) Run 2" to 3" (5 to 7.5 cm) tail chain. Place garment pieces, right sides together, under front of presser foot; it is not necessary to lift presser foot.

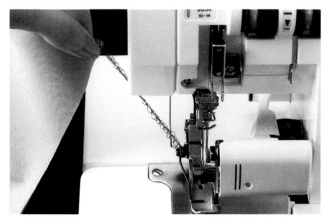

2) Guide fabric as you serge. Run 4" to 6" (10 to 15 cm) tail chain at end of seam.

3) Cut tail chain, using knives, bringing tail chain under front of presser foot as you continue to run the serger. Or, use scissors.

Alternate method. Run 2" to 3" (5 to 7.5 cm) tail chain. Lift presser foot; place thick fabric or layers that shift under presser foot up to knives. Lower presser foot. Serge seam. Run 4" to 6" (10 to 15 cm) tail chain at end; cut tail chain, as in step 3, left.

How to Sew Intersecting Seams

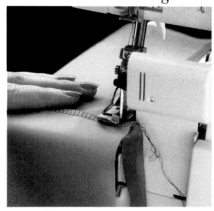

Intersecting seam. Trim tail chain with knives as you stitch across an intersecting seamline.

Reinforced intersecting seam. 1) Stop 2" (5 cm) before you meet a previous seam. Clip into seam allowances of previous seam for ¼" to ⅜" (6 mm to 1 cm) on each side of stitches.

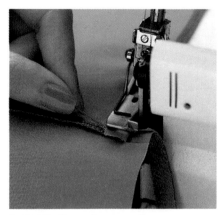

2) Fold clipped seam allowance away from knives, toward seam. Continue sewing past previous seam, not cutting the folded seam allowance.

How to Sew Circular Edges

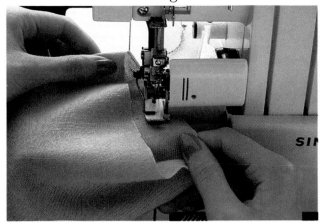

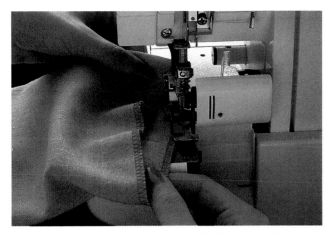

1) Stitch onto edge of fabric at an angle. Straighten fabric in front of knives as you sew. Stitch parallel to edge of fabric.

2) Overlap previous stitches for 1" (2.5 cm). Stitch off edge of fabric at an angle or by clearing stitch fingers, as in either step 2, below.

How to Restitch Part of a Seam

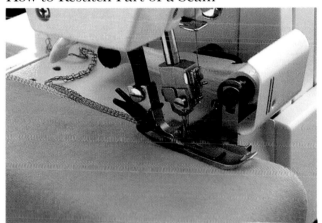

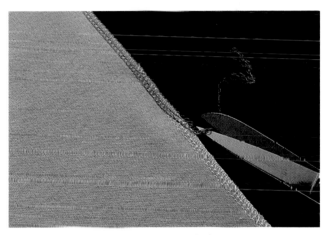

1) Stitch onto edge of fabric at an angle, starting back 2" (5 cm) from end of previous stitching. Straighten fabric when needle enters fabric exactly on previous seamline to prevent a dip at seamline.

2) Sew to end of area to be restitched; overlap stitching 1" (2.5 cm). Stitch off the edge of fabric at an angle. Trim the tail chain close to stitching. (Contrasting thread has been used to show detail.)

Alternate method. 1) Clear stitch fingers (pages 40 and 41). Place fabric under presser foot, lowering needle into fabric at seamline, so stitches will overlap previous stitching 1" (2.5 cm). Lower presser foot.

2) Sew to end of area to be restitched; overlap stitching 1" (2.5 cm). Clear stitch fingers. Run tail chain, and trim close to stitching.

Securing Tail Chains

In garment construction, tail chains are trimmed away at intersecting seams, as on page 36. T-shirts serged using the flat method of construction and garments with a prefinished hemline, such as an eyelet border or scalloped lace, will require the tail chain to be secured so it does not show at the end of a seam.

Because overlocks or sergers cannot backstitch, keep stitches from raveling by using one of several methods for securing tail chains. An easy method uses a tapestry needle to hide the tail chain, left. For this method, you may want to smooth out the loops in the tail chain, using your fingers, before threading the tail chain through the large eye of a tapestry needle. Weave the needle under the overlocked stitches for 1" or 2" (2.5 to 5 cm). Cut off the rest of the tail chain for a neat finish.

You may use a loop turner to secure the tail chain, or secure the stitches at the end of the seam with liquid fray preventer. While these methods are easy, they require more time than the overlock method, at right.

How to Secure Tail Chains Using Liquid Fray Preventer or Loop Turner

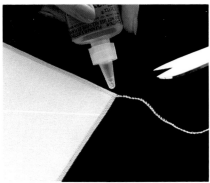

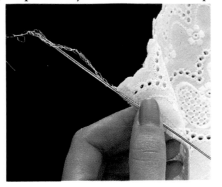

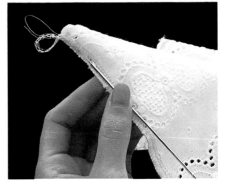

Liquid fray preventer. Apply liquid fray preventer to stitches at end of seam. Allow to dry; cut tail chain close to stitches.

Loop turner. 1) Smooth out loops in tail chain, using fingers. Insert loop turner under stitches 1" or 2" (2.5 to 5 cm) from end of seam. Catch ends of tail chain with latch hook of loop turner.

2) Pull tail chain under stitches, using loop turner. Cut off excess tail chain.

How to Secure Tail Chains Using the Overlock

Starting a seam. 1) Stitch seam for one or two stitches. Raise presser foot and needle. Clear stitch fingers (pages 40 and 41). Run fingers along tail chain to smooth out loops. (Presser foot has been removed to show detail.)

2) Bring tail chain to the left, around and under presser foot. Place tail chain between needle and knives. Lower presser foot, holding tail chain in position.

3) Stitch scam over tail chain for about 1" (2.5 cm). Then, swing tail chain to the right, so it is trimmed off as you continue to stitch scam.

Ending a seam. 1) Stitch past end of seam by one stitch; stop. Raise presser foot and needle to clear stitch fingers (pages 40 and 41). (Presser foot has been removed to show detail.)

2) Turn fabric over, and align edge of seam with trimming edge of knives. Lower presser foot. Turn handwheel to insert needle at end of seam and to the left of trimmed edge, the width of stitch.

3) Stitch over previous stitching for about 1" (2.5 cm). Stitch off edge, leaving tail chain. Using scissors or knives, cut tail chain close to edge of seam.

Clearing the Stitch Fingers

The serger forms its stitches around one or two stitch fingers located on the needle plate, as shown left. Occasionally, it is necessary to remove the stitches from the needle plate; this is referred to as clearing the stitch fingers.

Clear the stitch fingers before changing the needle plate on the serger. Also, when you turn outside corners, the stitch fingers must be cleared because stitches are always left chained around the stitch fingers at the end of the seam.

How to Clear the Stitch Fingers

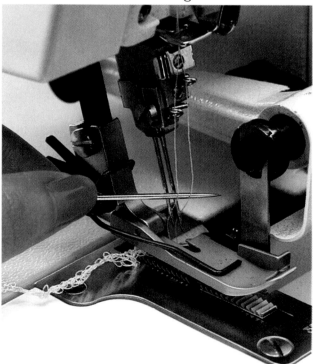

1) Lift the presser foot, and raise the needle or needles. Pull about ½" (1.3 cm) of slack in each needle thread just above needles.

2) Pull on tail chain to release stitches from stitch fingers. Correct amount of slack pulled in needle threads, step 1, allows tail chain to barely slide off stitch fingers. (Presser foot has been removed to show detail).

Avoiding Common Problems

To avoid loop. Do not pull too much slack in the needle threads at end of seam.

To avoid extra threads. Stop right at the edge of the fabric. If you stitch a few stitches beyond the edge, there will be extra threads at the end of the seam.

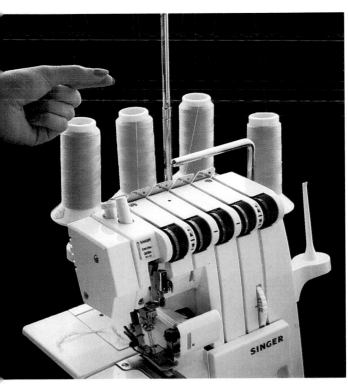

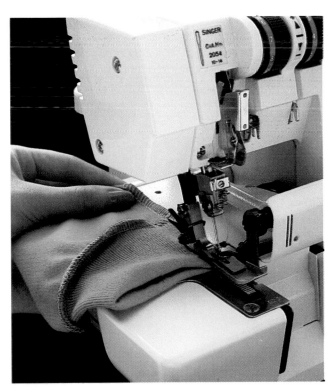

3) Tug on all threads near telescope until threads are taut, if too much slack has been pulled.

End of a seam. Lift presser foot and pull slack in needle threads, as in step 1, opposite. Pull back on fabric to release stitches from stitch fingers.

Curves & Corners

Special methods are used for stitching curves, such as facings, necklines, and armholes, and corners, such as kick pleats and plackets. When you are sewing curves, the long presser foot prevents the fabric from being turned abruptly. On inside corners, the knives trim up to the corner before the needle stitches to it.

And on outside corners, fabric cannot be pivoted, because threads are chained around the stitch fingers.

Practice these methods, shown below, on trial scraps of fabric; then serge placemats and napkins as a fast and easy project.

How to Stitch a Curved Edge

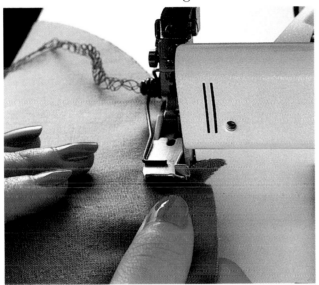

Outside curve. 1) Begin trimming at an angle, until desired trimming or stitching position is reached.

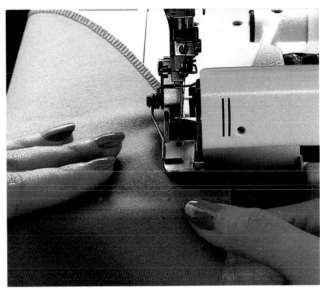

2) Stitch, guiding fabric by moving it to the right in front of presser foot; watch knives, not needle. Lift presser foot, as necessary, on tight curves to ease fabric under presser foot.

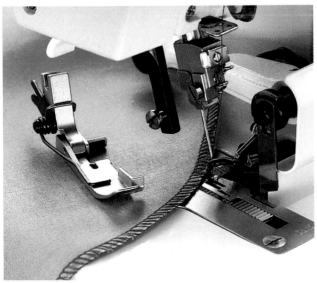

3) Overlap previous stitches for circular edges. Stop, and lift presser foot. Shift fabric so it is behind the needle; stitch straight off edge to prevent gradual looping over edge. (Presser foot has been removed to show needle position.)

Inside curve. Trim and stitch as for outside curves, above, guiding fabric by moving it to the left in front of presser foot. On circular edges, stitch off edge of fabric (page 37).

How to Stitch an Outside Corner

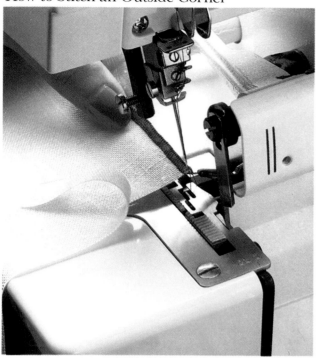

1) Stitch one side of fabric, trimming as desired; stop a few inches (2.5 cm) before corner. Trim away seam allowance on adjacent side for about 2" (5 cm). Or, cut fabric to finished size. Sew one stitch past end of the corner, and clear stitch fingers (pages 40 and 41). (Presser foot has been removed to show detail).

2) Pivot the fabric; align edge of trimmed seam allowance with knives. Insert needle at edge. Lower presser foot, and continue stitching. Stitches will overlap at corner. (Presser foot has been removed to show needle position.)

Alternate method. 1) Stitch one side of fabric. Start trimming adjacent side with knives; stop serging when needle takes first stitch on fabric. With needle down, lift presser foot and straighten corner by pulling fabric to the left at right angle.

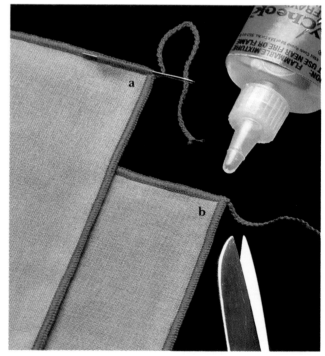

2) Lower presser foot; overlock, leaving 4" (10 cm) tail chains at ends. Secure tail chains (pages 38 and 39) by threading them under stitches using needle **(a)**; or by applying liquid fray preventer **(b)** at corners.

How to Stitch an Inside Corner or Slit

1) Finish seams by aligning raw edge of fabric with knives of serger. Stitch, stopping before corner or slit.

2a) Stitch inside corner, folding fabric to left to straighten edge. Stitch through corner; hold fabric in straight line. Once past corner, fabric can be relaxed.

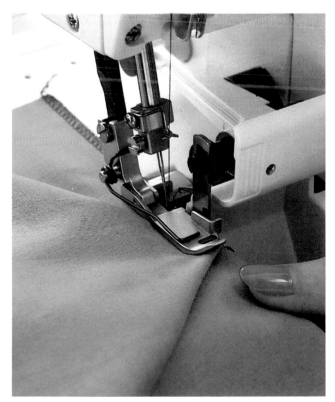

2b) Stitch slit by straightening edge of fabric; fold two folds to distribute fullness. Stitch, holding fabric in straight line.

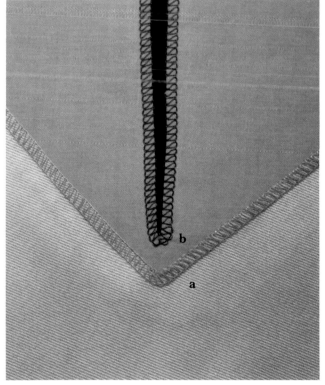

3) Press completed inside corner **(a)** or slit **(b)** flat. (Folds in step 2a or 2b are not caught in stitching.)

Removing Stitches & Jammed Fabric

Even if you are an experienced sewer, you may have to rip out stitches occasionally. Overlock stitches look intricate, but they are actually easy to remove. Also, fabric may become jammed in the machine, although this can usually be prevented. If a fabric jam does occur, the fabric can be safely removed from the machine without damage.

Removing Stitches

There are times when ripping stitches is unavoidable. After the stitches have been removed, remember that the excess seam allowance has already been trimmed away. When restitching the seam, guide the knives along the trimmed edge.

If the seam needs to be deeper, it is not necessary to remove the stitches first. Sew the new seam and trim away the original stitches in one step.

Removing Jammed Fabric

Thick fabrics that do not feed into the small opening of the knife blades cause the fabric to bunch up at the knives and not feed through the overlock. The fabric may need to be compressed prior to sewing by stitching along the edge of the fabric, using a straight or zigzag stitch on a conventional machine. If the stitch length is too short, the fabric does not feed through the overlock properly. Gradually lengthen the stitch until the fabric feeds through the machine.

If the tail chain becomes tangled in the stitching or in the moving parts of the machine, the fabric jams under the presser foot. Always leave a tail chain at least 6" (15 cm) long after completing a seam. Also, do not allow trimmings to fall into the machine; they may catch on the loopers and cause a jam.

When removing a fabric jam, take care not to damage the machine or the fabric. Pulling hard or yanking on the jammed fabric causes the machine loopers to bend or the fabric to be damaged, but does not release the jam. It is important that you stop sewing as soon as you realize the fabric is not feeding into your overlock well and a fabric jam is starting to occur.

There are two methods for removing fabric jams. If it is possible to rotate your needle out of the fabric, follow the instructions for the needle-up method (page 49). In a more serious fabric jam, the needle is jammed in the fabric and cannot be moved; follow the instructions for the needle-down method (page 49).

How to Remove Chainstitches

1) Pull looper thread out of the last loop in the stitch at the end of the seam, using a pin; work from the underside of the fabric.

2) Bring needle thread through to upper side of fabric; gently pull looper thread to unravel stitches.

How to Remove Overlock Stitches

1) Locate the thread for each needle by smoothing out the loops in the tail chain. The needle threads are the shortest threads in the chain. (For 2-thread or 3-thread stitches, there is only one needle thread.)

2) Hold the needle threads, and push the excess tail chain stitches close to the fabric at the end of the seam.

3) Pull the needle threads, gently easing the fabric until the needle threads can be removed.

4) Remove the looper threads.

Alternate method. Cut one of the looper threads by sliding a seam ripper along the stitches. Pull remaining needle and looper threads out of the fabric.

How to Remove a Fabric Jam (needle up)

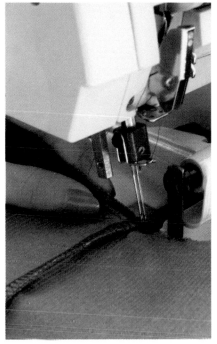

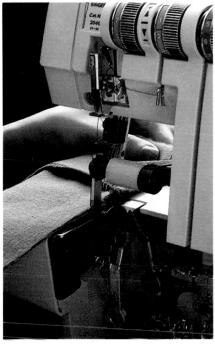

1) Cut the needle threads. Remove the presser foot.

2) Tug gently on fabric, pulling to the back of the machine. If fabric does not come out easily, cut the looper threads close to the fabric.

3) Pull fabric from machine gently. Use seam ripper to remove stitches from the fabric. Rethread serger; replace presser foot.

How to Remove a Fabric Jam (needle down)

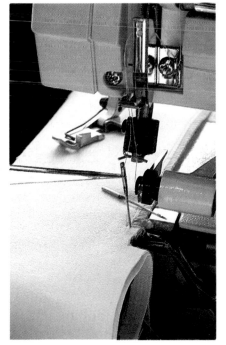

1) Loosen the needle set screws. Raise the needle bar by turning the handwheel. (Needles will remain in the fabric.)

2) Remove the presser foot. Cut needle and looper threads close to fabric. Pull needle out of fabric using tweezers or fingers.

3) Pull fabric to back of machine to remove it. Use a seam ripper to remove stitches from the fabric. Remove threads from under lower looper, if necessary. Insert new needle. Rethread serger; replace presser foot.

Adjusting the Stitches

Stitch width

Stitch length

Stitch Length & Width

It is important to check the stitch length and width for each fabric you sew by testing the stitches on a fabric scrap. The stitch length and width settings are comparable to the zigzag settings on the conventional machine. The same general principle of conventional sewing applies to serging; use shorter, narrower stitches for lightweight fabrics, and use longer, wider stitches for heavyweight fabrics. After changing stitch length or width on the overlock, you may need to adjust the tensions, especially if the amount of change is significant.

Stitch Length

The stitch length is the distance in millimeters between the needle penetrations. The stitch length can be as short as 1 mm or as long as 5 mm. The stitch length is changed with a regulator dial or lever, depending on the model. Check the instruction manual for the location and the method of adjustment on your serger.

If the stitch length is too long, the stitches may pucker and the seams may not be strong enough to hold up under the stress of wearing the garment. A stitch length that is too short can weaken the seam in some fabrics, such as taffeta; the needle holes are too close together, and the needle perforates the fabric, causing the fabric to pull away from the stitches.

Fabric jams can occur if the stitch length is too short. Fabric does not feed properly through the machine, and stitches build up on the stitch finger. Correct a fabric jam as on page 49.

Stitch Width

The stitch width is the distance in millimeters between the needle thread and the trimmed edge of the fabric; if the overlock has two needles, the stitch width is the distance from the left needle to the trimmed edge. The stitch width can be as narrow as 1.5 mm or as wide as 7.5 mm, depending on the model; some models have little or no variation in stitch width, which will limit the types of seams you can sew. On some 4/3-thread machines you can only adjust the stitch width by eliminating the left needle to sew a 3-thread overlock seam that is narrower.

Follow the instruction manual to change the stitch width. For some sergers, turn a dial to adjust the stitch width; for others, change the needle plate.

If the stitch width is too narrow, seams are not durable, and heavyweight fabrics do not press flat to one side. If the stitch width is too wide, stitches on lightweight fabrics may pucker.

Recommended Stitch Lengths and Widths

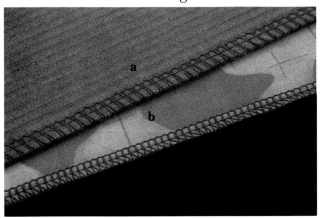

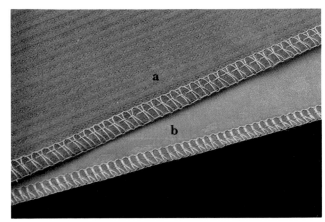

Stitch length. Use longer stitches (4 to 5 mm) on heavyweight fabrics (**a**); use shorter stitches (2 to 2.5 mm) on lightweight fabrics (**b**).

Stitch width. Use wider stitches (5 to 7.5 mm) for heavyweight fabrics (**a**); use narrower stitches (3.5 to 5 mm) for lightweight fabrics (**b**).

Stitch Length Problems

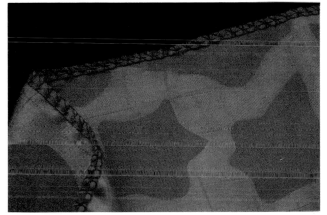

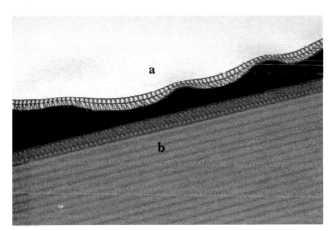

Stitch length too long. Seams on lightweight fabrics may pucker lengthwise, and stitches may show on right side of fabric.

Stitch length too short. Seams may be weakened and perforated on fragile fabrics, and edges may stretch out of shape on outside curves (**a**). Seams may be too bulky on heavyweight fabrics (**b**), so fabric does not feed through serger easily.

Stitch Width Problems

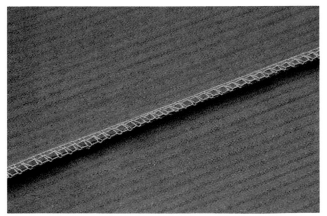

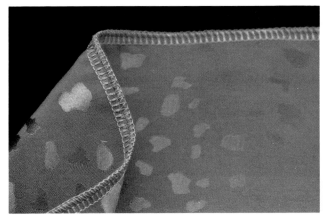

Stitch width too narrow. Seam may not be strong enough for heavyweight fabrics and may not press flat. On loosely woven fabrics, seam may ravel.

Stitch width too wide. Seams on lightweight fabrics may pucker under the stitches because wide stitches are too heavy for the fabric.

Adjusting Tension

Tension should be adjusted properly when sewing with an overlock. If the stitch is not correct, check for proper threading before turning the tension dial. Even if only one thread has slipped out of a thread guide, it can appear that the tension needs adjusting. If a machine that has been sewing with correct tension has poor tension after the thread is changed, check the threading before adjusting tension dials.

When learning how to adjust the tension, thread the machine with colors of thread that match the color coding on the machine. This helps you to visualize and understand each thread path and how the threads interact with each other.

Practice Turning Tension Dials

When the overlock stitch has poor tension, only one thread may need adjustment. Learning to adjust the correct thread or threads takes practice.

Overlocks have the tensions preset at the factory for basic seaming. If the machine has numbered tension dials, write down preset numbers before practicing.

Although these factory settings will not give perfect tension for all fabrics, they do provide a good point of reference, especially for a beginner.

Practice adjusting the tensions by sewing on a long strip of fabric. Start sewing, and slowly turn the tension dial for one of the threads to a lower number. As you sew, examine the stitches to see the change in the tension. The thread that has been adjusted will be slack or loose.

As you sew, slowly return the tension dial to the original setting. Continue to sew, turning the same tension dial to a higher number. While tightening the dial, examine the sample again to see how the tension has changed. The fabric puckers when one of the threads is too tight. Continue to turn tension dials, one at a time, to see how each thread affects the stitch.

When tension is correctly adjusted for a *balanced stitch*, two opposing threads lock together at the edge of the fabric. Compare your stitch to the pictures on pages 56 to 67 if you are uncertain about which tension dials need adjusting.

Tips for Adjusting Tension

3-thread overlock and 4-thread mock safety stitch

If fabric puckers lengthwise, one or both needle threads are too tight.

If fabric puckers crosswise under stitches, one or both looper threads are too tight.

If a looper thread can be moved easily or if it appears uneven, the looper thread is too loose.

If a needle thread forms loose loops on the underside of the fabric or if the seam pulls open, the needle thread is too loose.

If threads lock on upper side of fabric, either the upper looper threads are too tight, pulling to the upper side, or the lower looper threads are too loose, spilling over the edge.

If threads lock on underside of fabric, either the lower looper threads are too tight, pulling to the underside, or the upper looper threads are too loose, spilling over the edge.

2-thread chainstitch

If fabric puckers, one or both threads are too tight. Adjust each dial separately to determine which thread needs to be loosened.

If either thread can be moved easily or appears uneven, it is too loose.

2-thread overedge stitch

If fabric puckers, one or both threads are too tight.

If either thread can be moved easily or appears uneven, it is too loose.

If threads lock on upper side of fabric, either the looper thread is too tight, pulling to the upper side, or the needle thread is too loose, spilling over the edge.

If threads lock on underside of fabric, either the needle thread is too tight, pulling to the underside, or the looper thread is too loose, spilling over the edge.

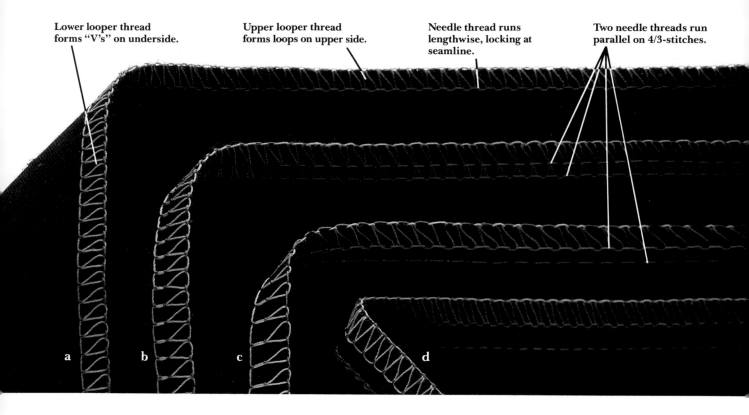

Lower looper thread forms "V's" on underside.

Upper looper thread forms loops on upper side.

Needle thread runs lengthwise, locking at seamline.

Two needle threads run parallel on 4/3-stitches.

a   b   c   d

3-thread, 4-thread & 5-thread Stitches

The 3-thread overlock and 4-thread mock safety stitches are adjusted the same way. The overlock stitch (a) uses one needle to secure the stitches, and the mock safety stitch uses two needles. There are two types of mock safety stitches; on one, the lower looper thread locks at the left needle thread (b), and on the other, at the right needle thread (c), depending on the model. Both 3-thread overlock and 4-thread mock safety stitches are suitable for seaming wovens. Because these

stitches stretch, they are also ideal for knits. The extra needle thread in the mock safety stitch makes it stronger than the overlock stitch.

On 5-thread overlocks, the 5-thread safety stitch (d) is made up of a 3-thread overlock stitch and a 2-thread chainstitch. To adjust the chainstitch, refer to page 58. Use the 5-thread safety stitch for sewing woven fabrics or stable knits.

Tension Adjustments (3-thread overlock and 4-thread mock safety)

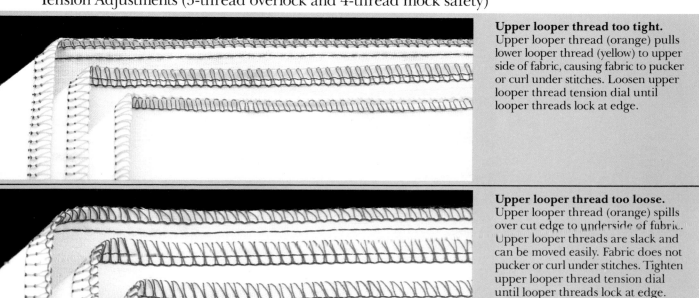

Upper looper thread too tight.
Upper looper thread (orange) pulls lower looper thread (yellow) to upper side of fabric, causing fabric to pucker or curl under stitches. Loosen upper looper thread tension dial until looper threads lock at edge.

Upper looper thread too loose.
Upper looper thread (orange) spills over cut edge to underside of fabric. Upper looper threads are slack and can be moved easily. Fabric does not pucker or curl under stitches. Tighten upper looper thread tension dial until looper threads lock at edge.

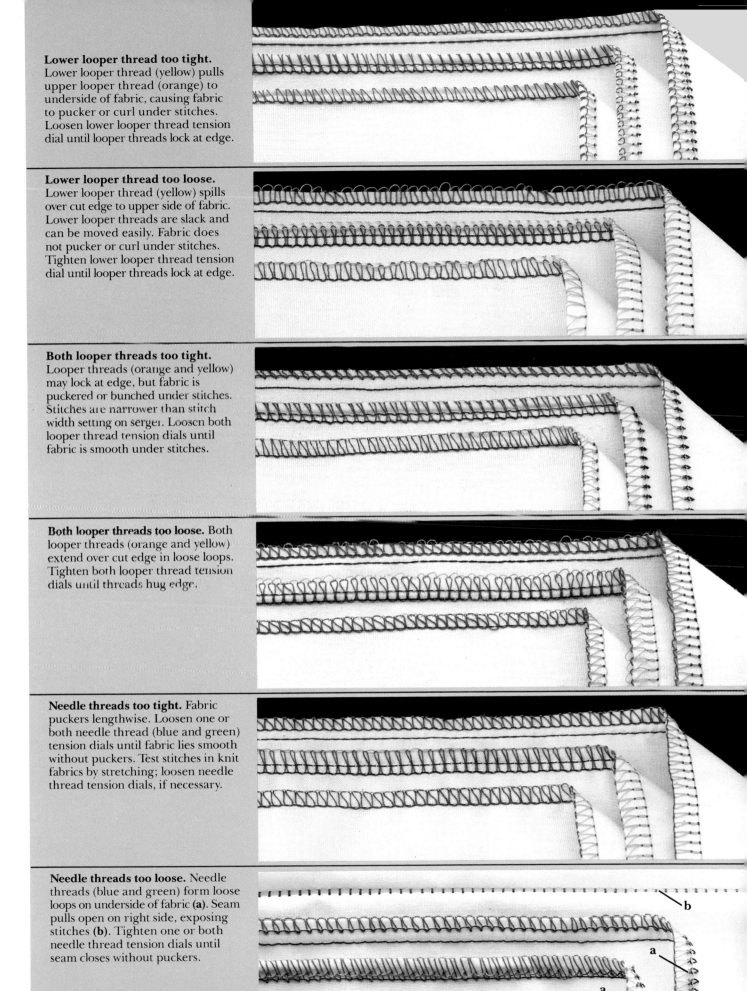

Lower looper thread too tight. Lower looper thread (yellow) pulls upper looper thread (orange) to underside of fabric, causing fabric to pucker or curl under stitches. Loosen lower looper thread tension dial until looper threads lock at edge.

Lower looper thread too loose. Lower looper thread (yellow) spills over cut edge to upper side of fabric. Lower looper threads are slack and can be moved easily. Fabric does not pucker or curl under stitches. Tighten lower looper thread tension dial until looper threads lock at edge.

Both looper threads too tight. Looper threads (orange and yellow) may lock at edge, but fabric is puckered or bunched under stitches. Stitches are narrower than stitch width setting on serger. Loosen both looper thread tension dials until fabric is smooth under stitches.

Both looper threads too loose. Both looper threads (orange and yellow) extend over cut edge in loose loops. Tighten both looper thread tension dials until threads hug edge.

Needle threads too tight. Fabric puckers lengthwise. Loosen one or both needle thread (blue and green) tension dials until fabric lies smooth without puckers. Test stitches in knit fabrics by stretching; loosen needle thread tension dials, if necessary.

Needle threads too loose. Needle threads (blue and green) form loose loops on underside of fabric **(a)**. Seam pulls open on right side, exposing stitches **(b)**. Tighten one or both needle thread tension dials until seam closes without puckers.

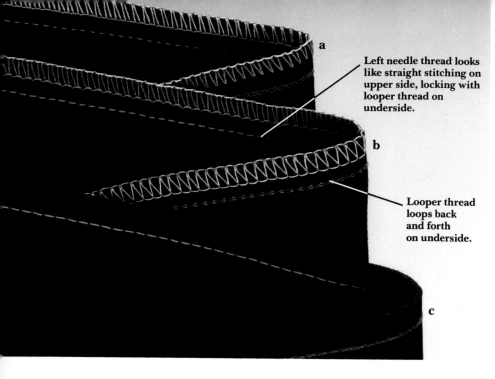

Left needle thread looks like straight stitching on upper side, locking with looper thread on underside.

Looper thread loops back and forth on underside.

Chainstitches

The 4-thread safety stitch (a) sewn on a 4/2-thread overlock is really two rows of stitches, stitched at the same time: the 2-thread chainstitch or *safety stitch*, below, and the 2-thread overedge, opposite.

The 5-thread safety stitch (b) sewn on a 5-thread overlock consists of two rows of stitches: the 2-thread chainstitch, and the 3-thread overlock stitch, pages 55 to 57.

The chainstitch (c) may be used alone for decorative topstitching, or for basting. As a basting stitch, it is especially convenient for fittings, because it is fast and easy to remove after fittings are done.

Tension Adjustments (chainstitches)

Lower looper thread too tight. Lower looper thread (purple) is tight and drawn on underside of fabric, causing puckered seam and skipped stitches. Loosen lower looper thread tension dial until even loops are formed. If problem is not solved, check for tight needle thread tension.

Lower looper thread too loose. Large, loose loops form in lower looper thread (purple), causing seam to pull open, exposing stitches on right side of fabric. Tighten lower looper thread tension dial until even loops form on underside.

Left needle thread too tight. Tight left needle thread (blue) may cause puckered seam and skipped stitches. Loosen left needle thread tension dial until fabric does not pucker. If problem is not solved, check for tight lower looper thread tension.

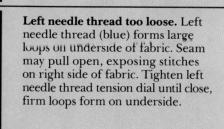

Left needle thread too loose. Left needle thread (blue) forms large loops on underside of fabric. Seam may pull open, exposing stitches on right side of fabric. Tighten left needle thread tension dial until close, firm loops form on underside.

2-thread Overedge Stitches

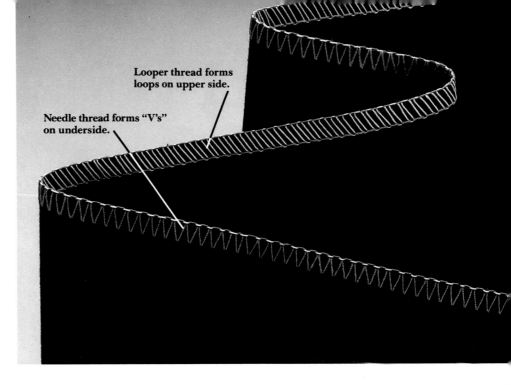

Looper thread forms loops on upper side.

Needle thread forms "V's" on underside.

The 2-thread overedge stitch is formed with one needle and one looper; depending on the model, either the upper or lower looper is used. Consult the instruction manual for specific instructions on the 2-thread stitch. Then adjust the tensions as shown, below.

The 2-thread overedge stitch is used as a lightweight seam finish. Because less thread is used for the stitches, they do not imprint on the right side of the fabric when pressed.

Tension Adjustments (2-thread overedge stitch)

Looper thread too tight. Looper thread (yellow) pulls needle thread (green) to upper side of fabric, causing fabric to pucker or curl under stitches. Loosen looper thread tension dial until threads lock at edge.

Looper thread too loose. Looper thread (yellow) spills over edge to underside of fabric. Tighten looper thread tension dial until threads lock at edge.

Needle thread too tight. Needle thread (green) pulls looper thread to underside of fabric. Loosen needle thread tension dial until threads lock at edge before pulling seam open.

Needle thread too loose. Slack needle thread (green) spills over edge to upper side of fabric. Loose threads may be uneven. Tighten needle thread tension dial until threads lock at edge.

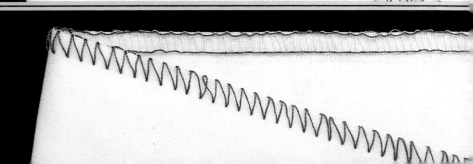

Flatlock Stitches

Flatlock stitching can be used decoratively for the look of applied trim on a garment. It may also be used to serge nonbulky seams on tricot. Decorative threads may be used in the serger for special effects; to learn how to serge with decorative threads, see pages 118 to 123.

Most models or brands of sergers are capable of creating flatlock stitches; however, the tension range of some sergers may be too limited to sew perfect flatlock stitches. Flatlock stitches are sewn with either two or three threads, depending on the model; some have the option of both 2-thread and 3-thread flatlocking. Refer to the instruction manual for specific directions for each model.

The 3-thread flatlock stitch is sewn with one needle, and upper and lower loopers. The 2-thread flatlock stitch is sewn with one needle and one looper; depending on the model, either the upper or lower looper is used.

To flatlock, first adjust the tension setting, as described on pages 61 to 63. The seam is then stitched and pulled apart to flatten the fabric layers at the seamline. Test the tension setting before pulling the fabric flat; it is easier to identify a stitch problem before fabric is pulled. If tension is not adjusted correctly, fabric will not pull flat.

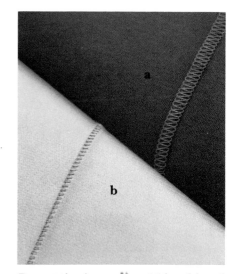

Decorative loop effect **(a)** is achieved when flatlock seam is stitched wrong sides together. For ladder effect **(b)**, stitch seam right sides together.

Tips for Adjusting Tension

2-thread flatlock stitch

Adjust stitch length as desired before adjusting tension.

Start with a 3-thread balanced stitch (pages 55 to 57) before adjusting tension for 2-thread flatlock; or use 2-thread overcast stitch (pages 55 and 59), which does not require further tension adjustments.

Loosen needle tension dial generously so needle thread extends to the edge of fabric on underside.

Loosen looper tension dial slightly, if necessary, to allow fabric to pull open flat.

3-thread flatlock stitch

Adjust stitch length as desired before adjusting tension.

Start with a 3-thread balanced stitch (pages 55 to 57) before adjusting tension for 3-thread flatlock.

Loosen needle tension dial generously so needle thread extends to the edge of fabric on underside.

Tighten lower looper tension dial generously so lower looper thread pulls into a straight line at edge of fabric.

Loosen upper looper thread slightly, if necessary, to allow fabric to pull open flat.

How to Flatlock a Seam (knit fabric)

1) Adjust tension for flatlock stitch. Serge the seam, trimming excess seam allowance.

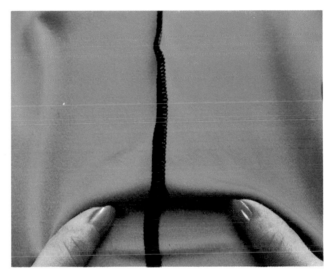

2) Pull crosswise on the seam, pulling stitches flat.

How to Flatlock a Seam (woven fabric)

1) Stitch seam using conventional machine; finish seam allowances using serger. Press seam open. Fold, *wrong* sides together, with seamline at fold; press.

2) Adjust tension for flatlock stitch. Serge the seam, with stitches half on and half off fabric; do not trim folds. Pull flat, as in step 2, above.

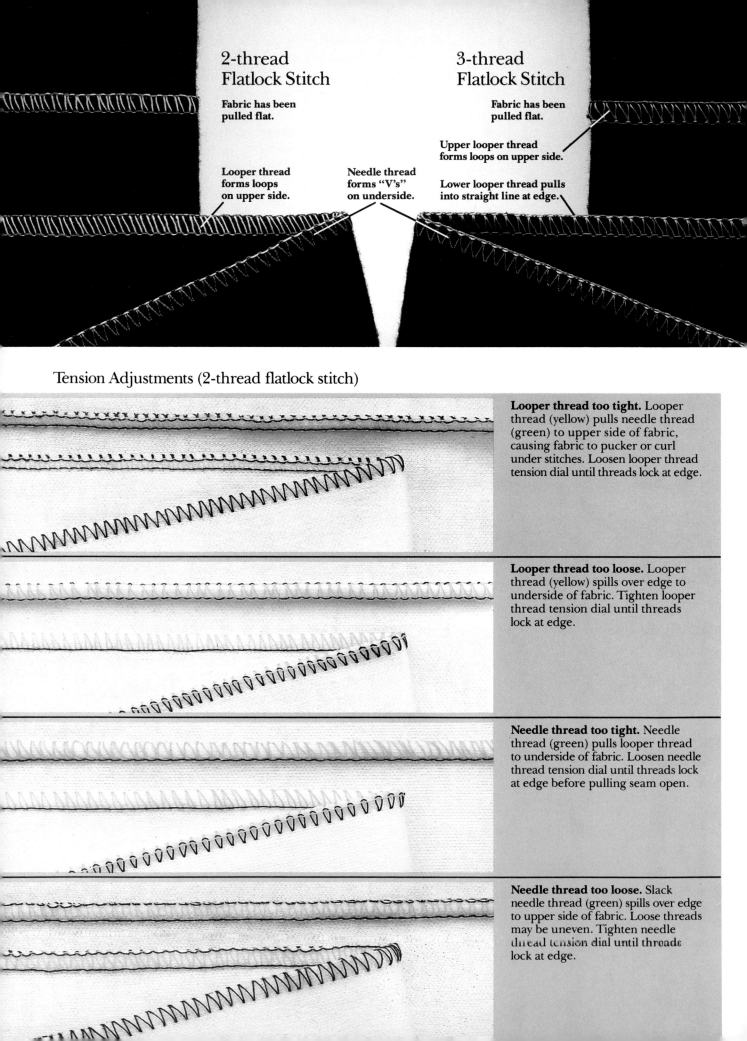

2-thread Flatlock Stitch

Fabric has been pulled flat.

Looper thread forms loops on upper side.

Needle thread forms "V's" on underside.

3-thread Flatlock Stitch

Fabric has been pulled flat.

Upper looper thread forms loops on upper side.

Lower looper thread pulls into straight line at edge.

Tension Adjustments (2-thread flatlock stitch)

Looper thread too tight. Looper thread (yellow) pulls needle thread (green) to upper side of fabric, causing fabric to pucker or curl under stitches. Loosen looper thread tension dial until threads lock at edge.

Looper thread too loose. Looper thread (yellow) spills over edge to underside of fabric. Tighten looper thread tension dial until threads lock at edge.

Needle thread too tight. Needle thread (green) pulls looper thread to underside of fabric. Loosen needle thread tension dial until threads lock at edge before pulling seam open.

Needle thread too loose. Slack needle thread (green) spills over edge to upper side of fabric. Loose threads may be uneven. Tighten needle thread tension dial until threads lock at edge.

Tension Adjustments (3-thread flatlock stitch)

Upper looper thread too tight.
Upper looper thread (orange) pulls needle thread (green) to upper side of fabric, causing fabric to pucker or curl under stitches. Loosen needle thread tension dial until threads lock at edge.

Upper looper thread too loose.
Upper looper thread (orange) spills over edge to underside of fabric. Upper looper threads are slack and can be moved easily. Fabric does not pucker or curl under stitches. Tighten needle thread tension dial until threads lock at edge.

Lower looper thread too tight.
Lower looper thread (yellow) draws into straight, pulled line, causing fabric to pucker lengthwise. Loosen lower looper thread tension dial until fabric does not pucker.

Lower looper thread too loose.
Lower looper thread (yellow) forms loops between needle thread (green) and upper looper thread (orange). Tighten lower looper thread tension dial until lower looper thread draws into a straight, smooth line; try woolly nylon thread in lower looper if tension does not tighten enough.

Needle thread too tight. Needle thread (green) pulls upper looper thread (orange) to underside of fabric, causing fabric to pucker or curl under stitches. Loosen needle thread tension dial until threads lock at edge.

Needle thread too loose. Needle thread (green) spills over edge to upper side of fabric. Needle threads are slack and can be moved easily. Fabric does not pucker or curl under stitches. Tighten needle thread tension dial until threads lock at edge.

Rolled Hem Stitches

Most overlocks can make a rolled hem stitch. Some models require additional accessories, such as a different needle plate, presser foot, or auxiliary tension dial; others have a built-in rolled hem feature.

The rolled hem stitch is sewn using either two or three threads, depending on the overlock model; on some models you may sew both 2-thread and 3-thread rolled hems. Refer to the instruction manual for specific directions for each machine.

A 3-thread rolled hem is suitable for most lightweight to mediumweight fabrics. A 2-thread rolled hem is preferred for fine, lightweight edge finishes on sheers and lightweight fabrics.

The stitch length adjustment is critical to the finished look of the rolled hem stitch. If the stitch length is too short, the stitching may be too heavy for lightweight fabrics, causing a stiffer edge; if too long, the fabric may pucker. Before sewing your project, practice stitching on fabric scraps. To achieve perfect rolled hem stitches, refer to the information below and on pages 66 and 67.

Tips for Rolled Hem Stitches

2-thread rolled hem stitch

Adjust stitch length to 1.5 or 2 mm setting for a soft edge finish.

Start with a balanced 3-thread overlock stitch (pages 55 to 57) or a 2-thread overedge stitch (pages 55 and 59) before adjusting tension for 2-thread rolled hem. Tension adjustments may be unnecessary or slight if starting with a balanced 3-thread overlock stitch.

Tighten needle thread tension dial to eliminate "V's" formed by needle thread on underside of fabric.

Loosen looper thread tension dial so looper thread rolls around edge to upper side of fabric.

3-thread rolled hem stitch

Adjust stitch length to under 1 mm for a filled-in edge finish that has body or stiffness; adjust stitch length to 2 mm for a softer edge finish that is less filled-in.

Start with a balanced overlock stitch (pages 55 to 57) before adjusting tension for 3-thread rolled hem.

Tighten lower looper thread tension dial so upper looper thread is pulled around the edge of the fabric to the underside for a rounded rolled hem.

Loosen upper looper thread tension dial in addition to tightening lower looper thread tension dial for a flat, less-rounded, rolled hem.

Loosen needle thread tension dial slightly if fabric puckers lengthwise, or stitch using taut sewing (page 106).

How to Sew a Rolled Hem

1) Adjust machine for rolled hem stitch, above and on pages 66 and 67. Hold tail chain at beginning of hem to keep it from curling into looper area.

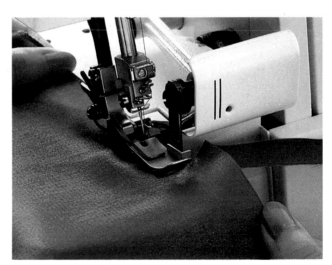

2) Stitch along hem edge, with right side of fabric facing up; trim away hem allowance. Use taut sewing (page 106), if necessary, to prevent puckering.

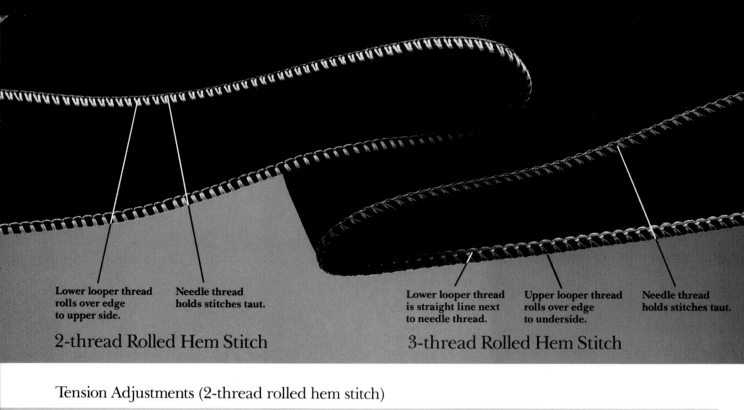

Lower looper thread rolls over edge to upper side.

Needle thread holds stitches taut.

2-thread Rolled Hem Stitch

Lower looper thread is straight line next to needle thread.

Upper looper thread rolls over edge to underside.

Needle thread holds stitches taut.

3-thread Rolled Hem Stitch

Tension Adjustments (2-thread rolled hem stitch)

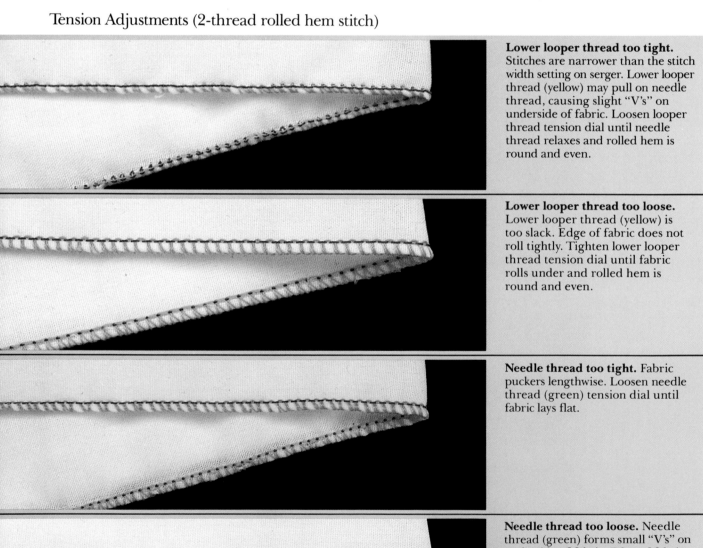

Lower looper thread too tight. Stitches are narrower than the stitch width setting on serger. Lower looper thread (yellow) may pull on needle thread, causing slight "V's" on underside of fabric. Loosen looper thread tension dial until needle thread relaxes and rolled hem is round and even.

Lower looper thread too loose. Lower looper thread (yellow) is too slack. Edge of fabric does not roll tightly. Tighten lower looper thread tension dial until fabric rolls under and rolled hem is round and even.

Needle thread too tight. Fabric puckers lengthwise. Loosen needle thread (green) tension dial until fabric lays flat.

Needle thread too loose. Needle thread (green) forms small "V's" on underside of fabric. Edge of fabric may not roll under. Tighten needle thread tension dial until "V's" are eliminated.

Tension Adjustments (3-thread rolled hem stitch)

Upper looper thread too tight.
Upper looper thread (orange) pulls lower looper thread (yellow) toward edge. Loops of upper looper thread are too short. Loosen upper looper thread tension dial until upper looper thread rolls completely around edge to underside of fabric.

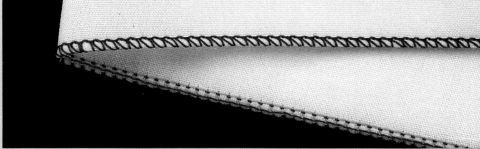

Upper looper thread too loose.
Upper looper thread (orange) is slack and can be moved easily. Tighten upper looper thread tension dial until upper looper thread rolls completely around edge to underside of fabric without slack.

Lower looper thread too tight.
Lower looper thread (yellow) draws into pulled, tight line, causing fabric to pucker lengthwise. Loosen lower looper thread tension dial until fabric does not pucker.

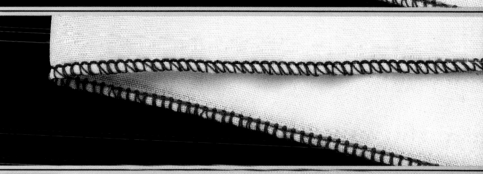

Lower looper thread too loose.
Lower looper thread (yellow) forms loops between needle thread (green) and upper looper thread (orange). Tighten lower looper thread tension dial until it draws into a straight, smooth line.

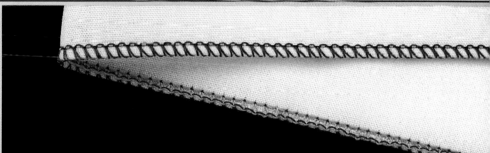

Needle thread too tight. Fabric puckers lengthwise. Loosen needle thread (green) tension dial until fabric does not pucker. It may be necessary to hold fabric taut when serging to prevent puckering, or use differential feed.

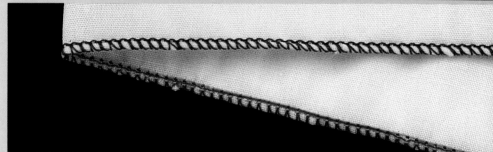

Needle thread too loose. Needle thread (green) forms small "V's" on underside of fabric. Edge of fabric may not roll under. Tighten needle thread tension dial until "V's" are eliminated.

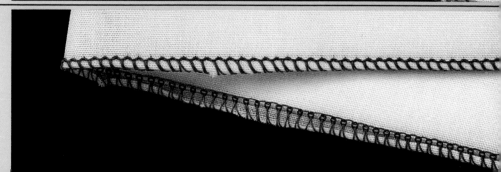

Seams & Seam Finishes

Overlock seams can be used for many garments. Refer to the chart on pages 16 and 17 for suggested applications and fabrics for the best use of each type of serged stitch. Garment style, fabric selection, and personal preference will help you decide which seams to use. The overlock seam alone is not always suitable for garment construction. Many seams are sewn with the combination of overlock and conventional machines. For example, pants, jackets, or garments requiring adjustable fit, or seams that will be subjected to a great amount of stress, should be sewn with a pressed-open conventional seam and overlocked seam allowances.

Types of Seams & Seam Finishes

Overlock seam finish (page 70) for conventional seam is used when it is desirable to keep the entire ⅝" (1.5 cm) seam allowance. It is the best choice for tailored garments sewn from wools, linens, and silk suitings. It is also recommended whenever fit is uncertain to allow for letting out seams.

Reinforced seam (page 70) is recommended for seams that will be stressed.

French seam (page 70) is used for sheers and loosely woven fabrics.

Rolled seam (page 70) may be used instead of French seams for sheers that are firmly woven and for laces.

Mock flat-fell seam (page 70) is used for denim and other heavyweight woven fabrics.

Reversible lapped seam (page 71) is used for reversible garments or for thick, loosely woven fabrics to provide added strength.

Gathered seam (page 71) looks best when sewn using a method that combines the use of the serger and the conventional machine.

Mock flatlock seam (page 72) is used for a decorative effect, with decorative thread used in the upper looper.

Flatlock on a fold (page 72) is used for the decorative effect of a flatlock seam on fabric that has been folded and stitched.

Types of Stabilized Seams

There are several methods for stabilizing seams in overlock garment construction. The type of fabric you are sewing and the desired effect will determine which method you choose.

Fusible stabilized seam (page 73) uses fusible interfacing strips to stabilize seams. Interfacing can also be used as a stable base for decorative edge finishes on stretchy knit or bias-cut fabrics.

Elastic stabilized seam (page 73) uses transparent elastic to allow full stretch and recovery in a serged seam, but prevents fabric from stretching out of shape.

Nonstretch stabilized seam (page 73) uses twill tape, seam tape, or ribbon to prevent stretching of the fabric at the seamline.

Slight-stretch stabilized seam (page 73) uses tricot bias binding to reinforce and stabilize a seam where slight stretch is desired. Use this method for stabilizing seams in sweater knits and T-shirt knits, which need support without completely restricting the stretch of the fabric.

Basic Seams and Seam Finishes

Overlock seam finish for conventional seam. Stitch 5/8" (1.5 cm) seam, right sides together, using conventional machine. Stitch seam allowances, slightly trimming raw edge, using overedge or overlock stitch.

Reinforced seam. Stitch 5/8" (1.5 cm) seam, right sides together, using conventional machine. Serge seam allowances together 1/8" (3 mm) from seamline.

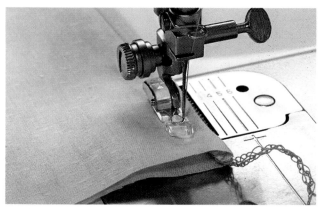

French seam. Overlock seam, wrong sides together, trimming seam allowance a scant 1/4" (6 mm). Fold the fabric, right sides together, enclosing the overlocked seam; press. Straight-stitch close to enclosed overlocked stitches using zipper foot on the conventional machine; press.

Rolled seam. Place fabric right sides together. Stitch seam, using rolled hem stitch (pages 65 to 67), with needle positioned on seamline; trim excess seam allowance. Press.

Mock flat-fell seam. 1) Place fabric right sides together. Stitch, using a conventional machine. Overlock seam allowances together, trimming slightly.

2) Press seam allowance toward one side; topstitch from right side next to seamline, using a conventional machine. Topstitch again, 1/4" (6 mm) away, through all layers

70

How to Sew a Reversible Lapped Seam

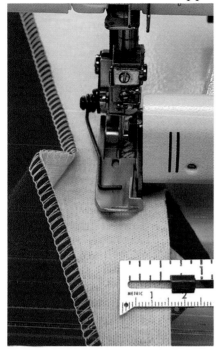

1) Stitch each single-layer seam allowance, using overedge or overlock stitch and aligning needle to seamline.

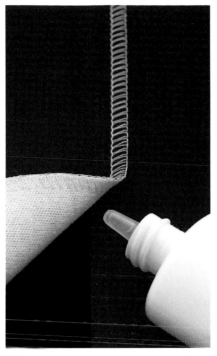

2) Lap garment sections so seamlines meet; glue-baste.

3) Straight-stitch through all layers ⅛" (3 mm) from overlock stitches, from both sides of garment, using conventional machine.

How to Sew a Gathered Seam

1) Sew seam allowance to be gathered, using overlock stitch, slightly trimming raw edge with knives. On conventional machine, stitch just inside ⅝" (1.5 cm) seam allowance, using long stitches.

2) Pin section with overlock edge to corresponding section, right sides together and raw edges even. Pull bobbin thread and overlock needle thread, gathering fabric evenly; adjust gathers to fit.

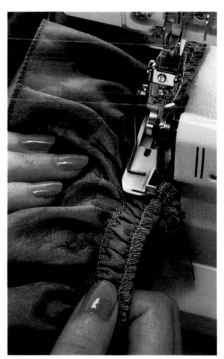

3) Stitch seam, using straight-stitch on conventional machine. Overlock seam allowances to finish seam, trimming away gathering stitches.

How to Sew a Mock Flatlock Seam

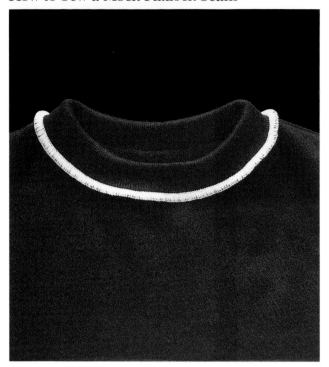

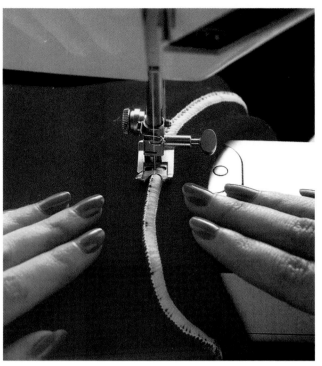

1) Use decorative thread (pages 120 and 121) in upper looper. Serge fabric, wrong sides together; press seam to one side with decorative thread on top.

2) Topstitch decorative serged seam through all layers, using conventional machine.

How to Flatlock on a Fold of Fabric

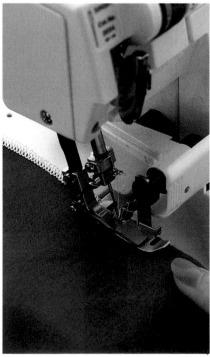

1) Mark stitch placement line on right side of fabric. Fold, *wrong sides together*, on marked line. Adjust serger for flatlock stitch (pages 60 to 63). Place fabric slightly to the left of knives.

2) Serge seam without trimming fold of fabric. Position stitches half on and half off fabric.

3) Open the fabric, and pull the stitches flat.

Stabilized Seams

Fusible stabilized seam. Cut ¾" (2 cm) strip of fusible knit interfacing the length of the seam. Fuse to wrong side of garment. Stitch seam.

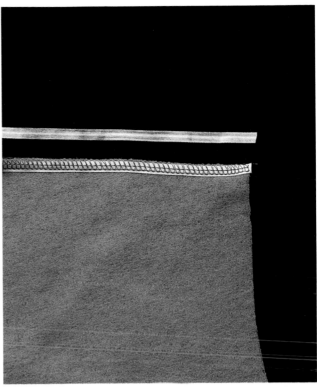

Elastic stabilized seam. Cut transparent elastic the length of the seam. Place elastic over seamline. Serge seam, stitching through elastic.

Nonstretch stabilized seam. Cut twill tape, seam tape, or ribbon the length of the seam; place over seamline. Stitch seam, stitching through tape.

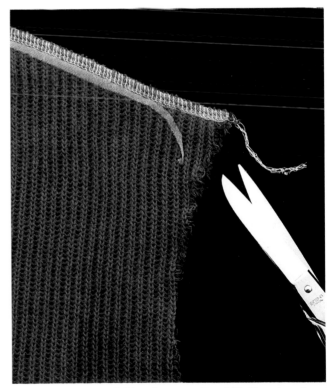

Slight-stretch stabilized seam. Cut ¾" (2 cm) strip of tricot bias binding the length of the seam. Serge through relaxed strip of tricot bias binding. Trim excess binding close to stitches.

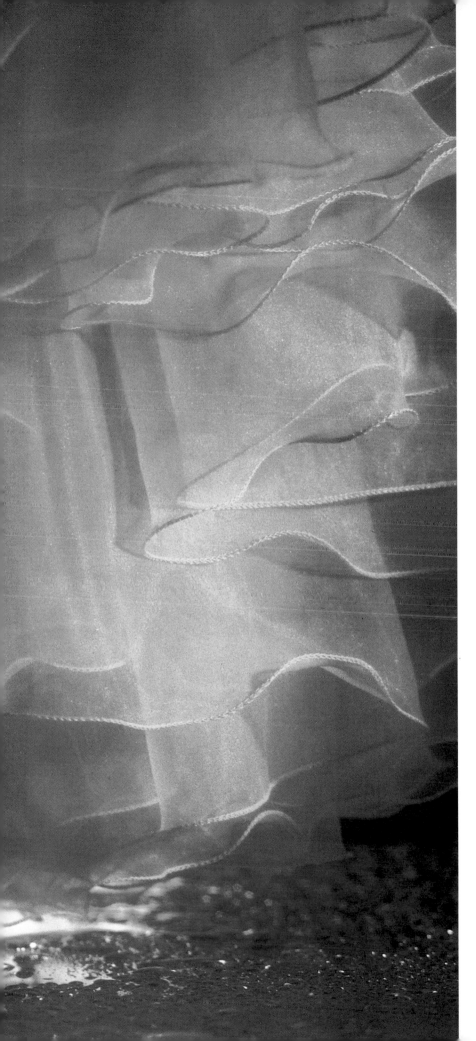

Hems

Overlocks create professional hem finishes on sheers, knits, or wovens. An overlock may be used for sewing hems on all types of garments, from sportswear to evening wear. In many cases, the overlock is used with the conventional sewing machine when sewing hems.

Overlocked and blindstitched hem (page 76) reduces bulk by using an overlocked finish instead of hem tape or a double-fold hem.

Overlocked and topstitched hem (page 76) also has an overlocked finish with the addition of topstitching as a detail.

Eased hem (page 76) is used on mediumweight to heavyweight fabric for flared or full hems.

Shirt-tail hem (page 76) is used to prevent a rippled edge on curved shirt hemlines.

Blind hem (page 77) is used for hems on many fabrics; it works best on textured knits because stitches will not show.

Sport hem (page 77) is used for a decorative application on sweatshirt fleece or T-shirt fabric.

Rolled hem (page 78) can be used to finish edges of scarves, ruffles, table linens, and some garments. It is suitable for lightweight to mediumweight fabrics, such as sheers, silkies, and broadcloth.

Lettuce hem (page 78) is an edge finish with a feminine touch. Use this decorative finish for ribbing on T-shirts, evening wear, swimwear, or aerobic wear. The fabric must be a knit or a bias-cut woven so the edge will "lettuce."

Fishline hem (page 78), shown at left, is used to add firmness and body to lightweight fabric flounces and ruffles. This hem adds a special effect to evening wear.

Fringed hem (page 79) uses a decorative flatlock stitch for detailing on scarves, shawls, and table linens.

Three Hems Using Overlock with Conventional Machine

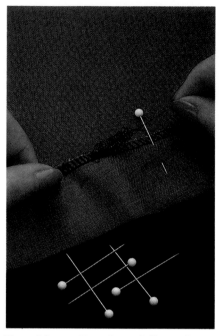

Overlocked and blindstitched hem. Mark hem allowance, and grade seams in hem area. Serge hem edge. Fold hem as for blind hem, step 2, opposite. Pin hem into position, and blindstitch, using a conventional machine, or by hand.

Overlocked and topstitched hem. Serge hem edge. Turn up hem. Topstitch from right side of garment, using conventional machine. Twin needle may be used for topstitching.

Eased hem. Ease hem fullness by pulling up needle thread. Or adjust differential feed to the ease setting, if differential feed is available on your machine. Pin hem into position; blindstitch, using a conventional machine, or by hand.

Two Ways to Sew a Shirt-tail Hem

Overlock to finish hem edge. Fold hem to wrong side of garment ⅛" (3 mm) beyond stitches; press. From right side, topstitch scant ¼" (6 mm) from fold, using single or twin needle on conventional machine.

Overlock to finish front and back edges of shirt before side seams are sewn. Fold up hem ⅛" (3 mm) beyond stitches; press. Sew side seams, stitching through pressed hems. Secure tail chains (pages 38 and 39). Topstitch, using single or twin needle on conventional machine; pivot at side seams.

How to Overlock a Blind Hem

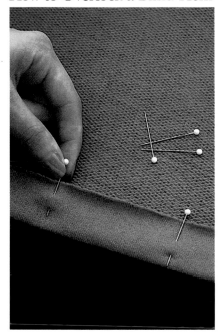

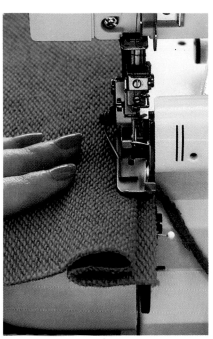

1) Adjust machine for flatlock stitch (pages 60 to 63). Set stitch length at 4 mm. Fold up hem, and press. On hem side of garment, place pins with heads toward body of garment.

2) Fold hem allowance back to right side of garment, with hem edge extending ¼" (6 mm) beyond fold. Stitch on extended hem edge, with needle *barely* catching fold; remove pins as you come to them.

3) Open hem, and pull fabric flat. Ladder of stitches shows on right side of lightweight fabrics, but is invisible on heavier textured fabrics.

How to Flatlock a Sport Hem

1) Adjust machine for flatlock stitch (pages 60 to 63). Fold up hem, and press. Fold up, and press again, enclosing raw edge; flatlock on fold (page 72), taking care to catch hem edge in stitches.

2) Open hem, and pull fabric flat. Lightly press. Decorative loops are on the right side of garment.

Rolled Hems

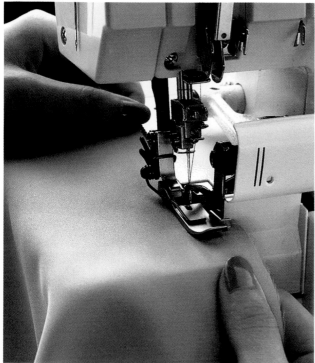

Rolled hem. Adjust machine for rolled hem stitch (pages 65 to 67). Hold tail chain at beginning of hem; stitch along hem edge, with right side of fabric facing up, trimming away hem allowance.

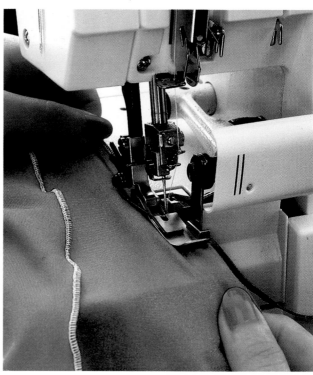

Lettuce hem. Adjust machine for rolled hem stitch (pages 65 to 67). Stitch along hem edge, with right side of fabric facing up; hold fabric stretched taut, and trim edge slightly.

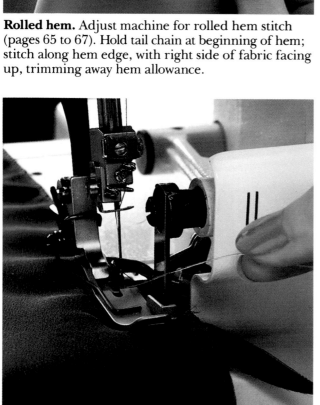

Fishline hem. 1) Adjust machine for rolled hem stitch (pages 65 to 67). Place 8 to 10-pound-test fishline under back of presser foot and over front of foot. Hold fishline to the right of needle as you stitch over it, trimming excess hem allowance.

2) Smooth out stitches, easing the stretched fabric over fishline.

How to Prevent Ragged Edges on Rolled Hems

1) Test-sew rolled hem. Fabrics, such as loosely woven, metallic, or stiff fabrics, may not roll under, which causes a ragged edge.

2) Place a strip of tricot bias binding on upper side of fabric edge to be hemmed. Serge edge of fabric, catching binding in stitching.

3) Trim excess tricot bias binding close to rolled hem stitches, using sharp embroidery scissors.

How to Flatlock a Fringed Hem

1) Mark stitch placement line, by pulling a thread or using a marking pen, to indicate depth of fringe. Press a crease on marked line. Adjust serger for flatlock stitch (pages 60 to 63). Stitch on fold, as in steps 1 to 3, page 72.

2) Cut fabric up to stitches on grain every 3" (7.5 cm). Remove threads to create fringe. If flatlocking corners, apply liquid fray preventer to intersecting stitches, and use seam ripper to remove stitches in fringe area.

Garment Construction

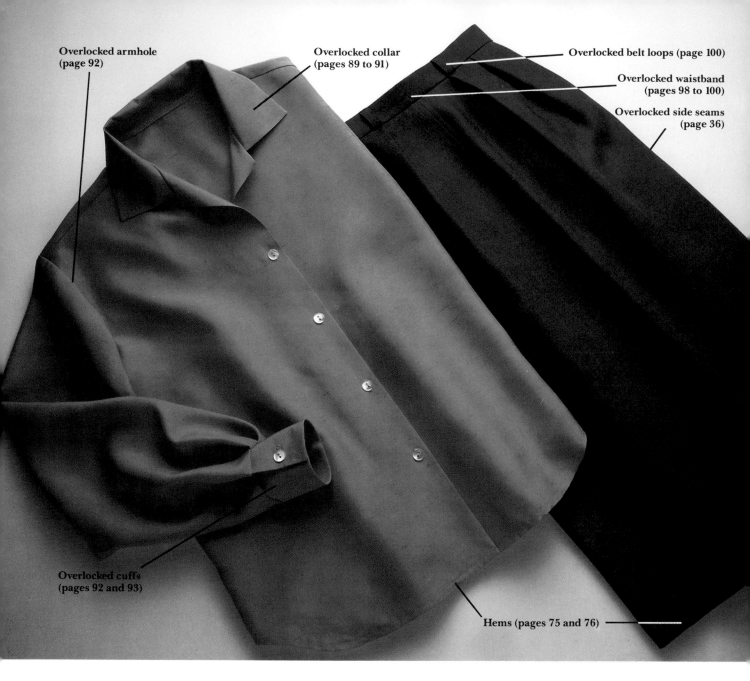

Overlocked armhole
(page 92)

Overlocked collar
(pages 89 to 91)

Overlocked belt loops (page 100)

Overlocked waistband
(pages 98 to 100)

Overlocked side seams
(page 36)

Overlocked cuffs
(pages 92 and 93)

Hems (pages 75 and 76)

Garment Construction

Special methods have been developed for using an overlock to sew many garment details. Depending on the style or the fabric, some garments may be sewn entirely on the overlock; others may also require the use of a conventional machine.

Before beginning a sewing project, read this section to decide which details can be serged and which should be sewn conventionally. Then review the pattern instruction sheet, and highlight areas that require change.

Garments requiring critical fitting adjustments are usually sewn on the conventional machine to allow room for adjustment in the seam allowances. When

overlocked seams are used, baste or pin-fit the garment before sewing the seams.

Topstitching with straight stitches is done using a conventional machine. The chainstitch on a 4/2-thread or 5-thread machine may be used for topstitching, although this stitch looks different on the upper and underside of the fabric. Zippers require straight-stitch topstitching, and are applied using the conventional machine.

Curves or corners that require clipping, such as enclosed neckline seams, are sewn using the conventional machine. Overlock stitches must not be clipped, or they will ravel.

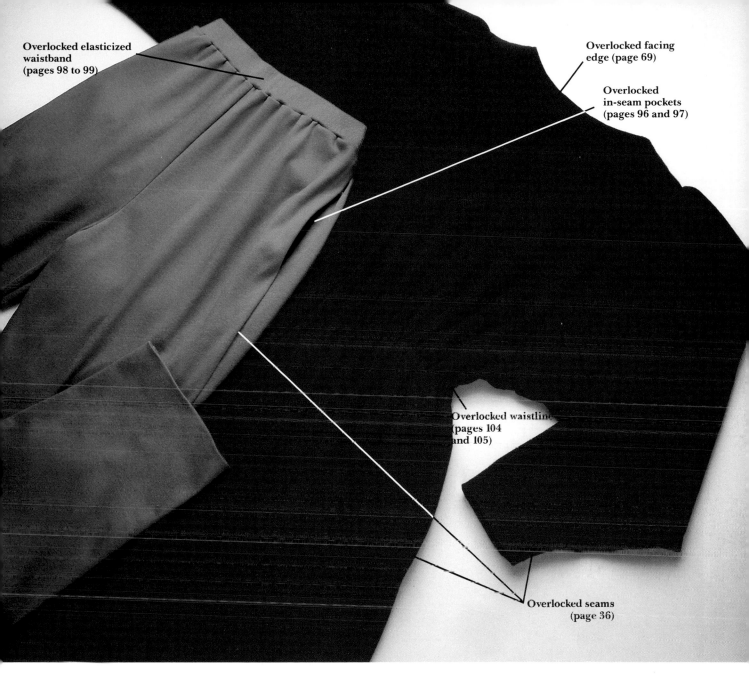

Overlocked elasticized
waistband
(pages 98 to 99)

Overlocked facing
edge (page 69)

Overlocked
in-seam pockets
(pages 96 and 97)

Overlocked waistline
(pages 104
and 105)

Overlocked seams
(page 36)

Seams with a side or back slit are sewn using the conventional machine, because the seam allowances must be pressed open to form the slit facing. Also sew buttonholes on a conventional machine.

Areas where precise stitch placement is required should be sewn using the conventional machine. The elongated presser foot can make it difficult to stitch details precisely. Jacket lapels, for example, are best stitched using a conventional machine.

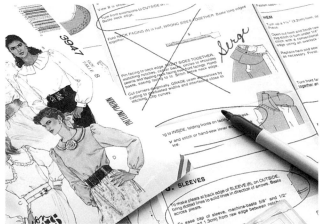

Review pattern instruction sheet before starting to sew. Mark instructions for garment details that can be overlocked, and circle the directions that require conventional methods.

Pullover Tops

A pullover top finished with ribbing is an ideal first project. This basic design can be varied in many ways, including fabric choices from basic knits to silk or challis. If using woven fabric, select a pattern with loose fit and a neckline seam measurement equal to or greater than the head measurement. By changing the finished length, you can also make a crop top or dress from the same basic design.

A cotton interlock knit is the easiest fabric to use for the front, back, and sleeve pieces. Select a coordinating or contrasting color in ribbing for the neck edge, cuffs, and band at the lower edge. Some T-shirt patterns are designed with ⅝" (1.5 cm) seams; others with ¼" (6 mm). Since the serger will automatically trim away excess seam allowances as it stitches, patterns with either seam allowance width can be used.

There are two methods for sewing a T-shirt or pullover top. The flat construction method is the fastest method; however, the seams may be noticeable at the edges of the ribbing. For a better-quality finish, use the in-the-round method. With this method, ribbing seams are enclosed for a neater appearance. You may want to try both methods to decide which one you prefer.

How to Sew a Pullover Top (flat method)

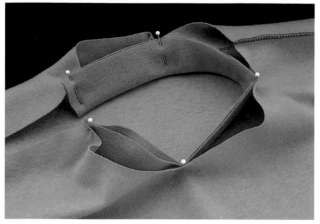

1) Stitch one shoulder seam. Fold neck ribbing in half lengthwise. Divide neck edge and ribbing into fourths; pin-mark. Pin ribbing to neckline, right sides together, matching pins.

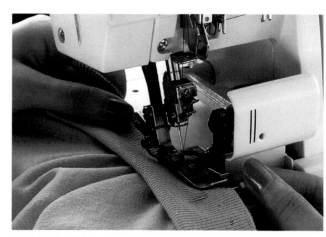

2) Stitch ribbing to neckline, stretching ribbing to fit; remove pins as you come to them.

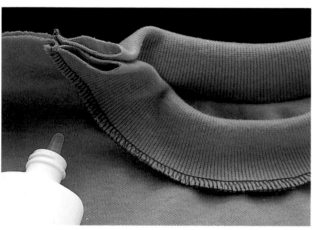

3) Glue-baste ribbing seam and between all layers at neck edge. Overlock shoulder seam, stitching toward neck edge. At neck edge, secure tail chain (pages 38 and 39).

4) Apply ribbing to sleeves, as for neckline ribbing, steps 1 and 2, above. Stitch sleeves into armholes. Glue-baste ribbing seam and between all layers at cuff edge.

5) Sew one side and sleeve seam from lower edge of garment to cuff edge. Secure tail chains at cuff edge.

6) Apply ribbing to lower edge, as for neckline ribbing, steps 1 and 2, above. Glue-baste and stitch remaining side and sleeve seam, securing tail chain at lower edge of garment and cuff.

How to Sew a Pullover Top (in-the-round method)

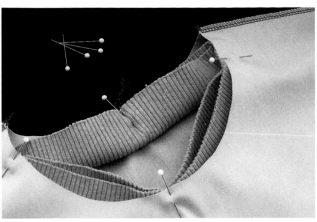

1) Stitch both shoulder seams. Sew ends of each ribbing piece, using an overlock or conventional machine. Fold overlocked seams in opposite directions at seamline, or press conventional seams open. Fold ribbing pieces in half lengthwise, wrong sides together.

2) Divide neckline edge and ribbing into fourths; pin-mark. Pin ribbing to neckline, right sides together, matching markings. Place ribbing seam in center back.

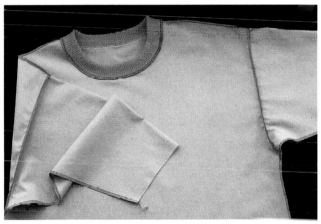

3) Stitch ribbing to neckline, stretching ribbing to fit; remove pins as you come to them. Press seam allowances at neckline toward body of garment. Edgestitch, if desired, using conventional machine.

4) Stitch sleeves into armholes. Sew one side and sleeve seam, from lower edge of garment to lower edge of sleeve, matching underarm seam. Repeat for other side and sleeve seam.

5) Divide sleeve edge and cuff ribbing into fourths; pin-mark. Pin cuff to sleeve edge, right sides together, matching ribbing seam to sleeve seam. Overlock, stretching ribbing to fit.

6) Divide lower edge of garment and ribbing into fourths; pin-mark. Pin ribbing to garment, right sides together, matching ribbing seam to one side seam. Overlock, stretching ribbing to fit.

Blouses

There are many timesaving methods for sewing blouses and shirts, even those with a convertible collar and set-in sleeves with cuffs.

Overlock seaming offers advantages beyond speedy construction. The seams in soft or silky fabrics are less likely to pucker when sewn on an overlock. On semi-sheers, the narrow seams are less conspicuous than pressed-open conventional seams. Overlocked seams also require less pressing to remain neat and flat after laundering.

As with any project, always test the stitch on scraps of the fabric before beginning to sew the garment itself. Adjust the stitch width and length until the seam is strong and pucker-free. If you are in doubt about whether the garment will fit correctly, baste the main garment pieces before serging the seams (page 34).

An overlock may be used for most of the blouse construction. Use a conventional sewing machine for areas with points to turn, for seams requiring grading, and for sewing on buttons and making buttonholes.

Collars

Overlocks or sergers may be used to stitch collar seams on gradual curves. This is especially helpful to prevent show-through of clipped and graded seam allowances on lightweight or sheer fabrics. Use a 3-thread overlock stitch for lightweight, flexible stitches. A 4-thread mock safety stitch should not be used for stitching collars together, but it may be used for applying collars.

Collars may be stitched on the overlock with exposed seams for a decorative effect. Use the rolled hem stitch and high-quality thread for beautiful stitches. A heavier thread, such as buttonhole twist, pearl cotton, or woolly nylon, can be used for exposed seams to create a piping effect on collars that are made from mediumweight fabrics.

Use a conventional machine to stitch collars that require grading and clipping. A conventional machine is always used to stitch enclosed seams on collars with points.

Interface collars and facings according to the fabric and pattern selected. Neck facings may be eliminated when applying collars with an overlock or a serger. For convertible collars, eliminate the back neck facing only. If facings are desired, finish the edges of the facings with a 2-thread overedge or 3-thread overlock stitch. The faced neckline seam may be serged unless the blouse has a neckline that requires trimming and clipping, such as a square or V neckline.

How to Prepare a Collar

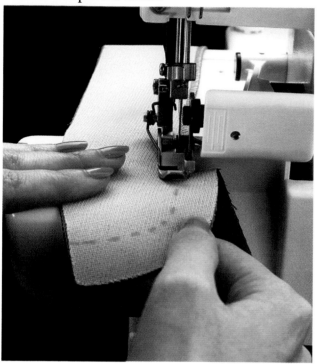

Enclosed seam. 1) Mark seamline on wrong side of collar for accurate stitching. Adjust serger for narrow balanced 3-thread stitch (pages 55 to 57). Adjust looper tensions so stitches hug edge of curve. Stitch collar pieces, right sides together, with needle on seamline.

2) Turn collar right side out. Press edge, using tip of iron to prevent seam imprint. Serged stitches flex to ease in fullness along curved edges, so clipping is unnecessary.

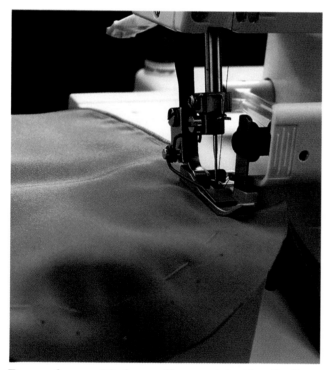

Exposed seam. Mark seamline on *right* side of collar for accurate stitching. Adjust serger for 3-thread rolled hem stitch (pages 65 to 67). Baste collar pieces, *wrong* sides together; serge, trimming away entire seam allowance.

Exposed seam with piping effect. Use topstitching thread or buttonhole twist in upper looper, and use regular thread in needle and lower looper. Mark seamline and serge, as for exposed seam, left.

How to Apply a Convertible Collar

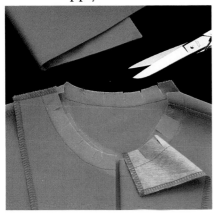 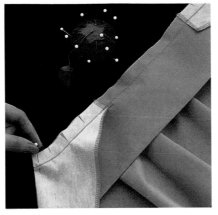 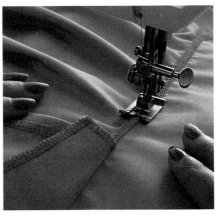

1) Stitch collar pieces, right sides together, using conventional machine. Grade seam allowances and collar points; clip. Turn collar right side out; press. Staystitch neck edge; clip to staystitching.

2) Pin collar to garment at neckline, right sides together, matching center back, shoulder seams, and center fronts. Fold front facings back on foldlines over ends of collar. Baste neckline. Remove pins.

3) Serge neckline seam, securing the tail chains (pages 38 and 39). If desired, understitch back of neckline through all layers, using conventional machine.

How to Apply a Flat or Stand-up Collar

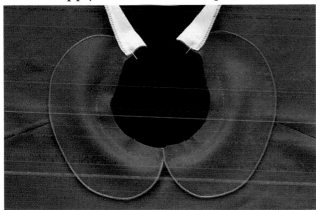 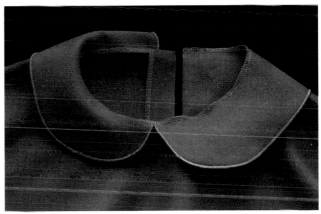

Flat collar. 1) Prepare collar, using serger or conventional method. Pin collar to garment at neckline, right sides up, matching markings; baste. Fold facings over ends of collar, right sides together.

2) Serge neckline seam, securing tail chains (pages 38 and 39). Turn facings to inside of garment; press.

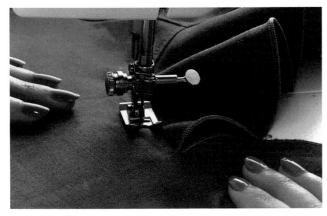 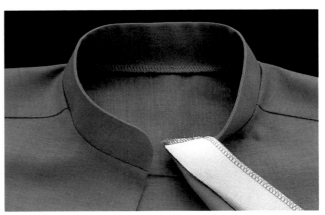

3) Lift collar; understitch on conventional machine, from right side, close to seamline, stitching through garment and seam allowances.

Stand-up collar. Follow steps 1 and 2 for flat collar, above. Press collar up.

Cuffs, Plackets & Sleeves

The slashed placket opening in a sleeve may be serged, which is faster and easier than sewing a continuous lap placket. This method may be used for a cuff with (**a**) or without (**b**) an underlap extension.

If your cuff pattern piece does not have an underlap extension, the slash opening may be eliminated to save even more time. For a cuff without a placket (**c**), the lower edge of the sleeve is then stitched to the cuff in one quick step.

For raglan or dropped-shoulder styles, the sleeve seam can be stitched on the overlock. For styles with standard set-in sleeves, it is recommended that you set in the sleeves according to the pattern instructions, using the conventional machine. Then stitch the armhole seam through both layers, ⅛" (3 mm) away from the conventional stitches, to finish the seams. The conventional machine gives you better control when stitching the eased sleeve seam. The extra row of stitching also adds strength, which is especially desirable in fitted garments that have set-in sleeves.

How to Sew a Cuff without a Placket

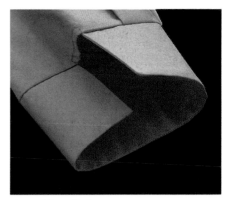

1) Stitch cuff, right sides together, using conventional machine; grade and clip seam allowances. Turn and press.

2) Prepare lower edge of sleeve, including gathers or tucks; mark, but do not slash, opening. Pin cuff to sleeve, placing ends ⅝" (1.5 cm) from slash mark. Serge seam.

3) Fold cuff down. Press seam toward sleeve. Hand-stitch or topstitch opening between ends of cuff.

How to Sew a Cuff with a Placket

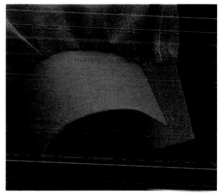

1) Stitch slash opening, as for slit (page 45). Fold, with right sides together and edges even. Using conventional machine, stitch 1" (2.5 cm) dart at end of slit. Stitch sleeve seam, and prepare lower edge of sleeve, including gathers or tucks.

2) Stitch cuff, using conventional machine; grade and clip seam allowances. Turn and press. Pin cuff to sleeve, right sides together; fold edges of slit opening over ends of cuff. Serge seam, securing tail chains (pages 38 and 39).

3) Fold cuff down. Fold and press edges of slit to inside. Press seam toward sleeve. For crisp edge, fuse ¼" (6 mm) strip of fusible web under folds of slit.

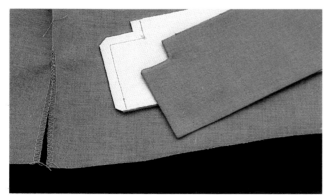

Cuff with underlap extension. 1) Prepare slit opening, as in step 1, above. Using conventional machine, stitch ends and underlap of cuff; pivot at dot, and stitch to raw edge. Grade and clip seam allowances. Turn and press.

2) Stitch sleeve seam, and prepare lower edge of sleeve, including gathers or tucks. Pin cuff to sleeve, right sides together, folding back underlap and folding edges of slit opening over ends of cuff. Serge seam. Finish cuff, as in step 3, above.

93

Assembling Blouses

Blouses may be constructed using both overlock and conventional sewing machines. For details that require conventional sewing methods, follow the pattern instruction sheet. Follow overlock methods for sewing collars, plackets, and cuffs, where appropriate to the style of the garment. The overlock can be used almost entirely for the construction of a traditional blouse that has a convertible collar and set-in cuffed sleeves, such as the blouse pictured here.

How to Sew a Blouse Using an Overlock

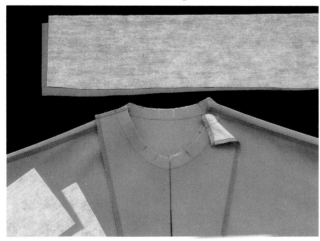

1) Apply interfacing. Staystitch and clip neckline. Finish facings. Stitch shoulder seams. If garment has raglan sleeves, stitch the sleeve seams. Press.

2) Prepare and apply collar, as on pages 89 to 91.

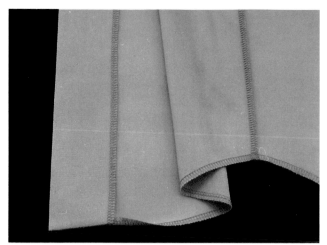

3) Stitch side seams. Fold facings to wrong side on foldlines. Serge lower edge of blouse, stitching through facings. Turn facings right side out.

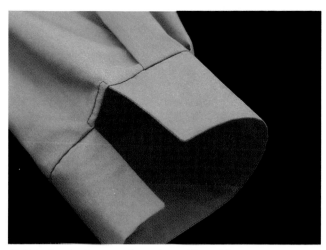

4) Stitch plackets and apply cuffs to blouse, as on pages 92 and 93.

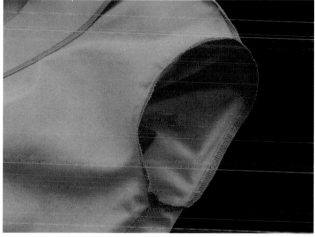

5) Set in sleeves using conventional machine, if garment has standard set-in sleeves. To finish seams, serge armhole seam, through both layers, ⅛" (3 mm) away from conventional stitching; press.

6) Turn up hem and topstitch in place.

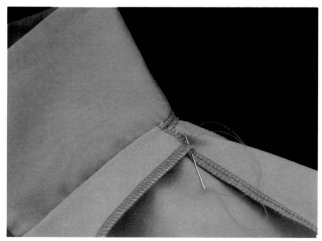

7) Tack front facings at shoulder seams of blouse.

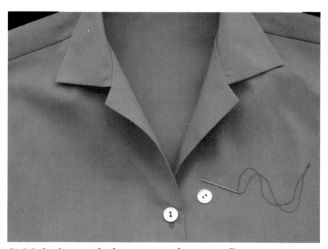

8) Make buttonholes; sew on buttons. Press garment.

Skirts & Pants

The weight of the fabric and the style of the skirt or pants will help you decide on the sewing techniques to use in construction.

Full skirts that are made from lightweight fabrics can be sewn almost entirely on the overlock. Because seams in full skirts are usually not subjected to a lot of stress, an overlock seam alone is sufficient. For fitted skirts or those made from heavier fabrics, use conventional seams with serged seam finishes, or use one of the special seams on pages 69 to 72.

In-seam pockets on full skirts, or on skirts or pants made from knits, may be attached using the overlock. For tailored skirts or pants, attach pockets following the conventional method, as directed in the pattern instruction sheet.

On a tailored skirt or pants, several areas require the use of a conventional machine instead of an overlock. Use the conventional machine for stitching seams whenever fittings are required, and for stitching seams that have a zipper opening, vent, or kick pleat. Also, heavier fabrics follow the body curves better when conventional seams are sewn; you may want to finish the seam allowances first with the overlock, while the garment sections are still flat.

Zippers require the full seam allowance for application and are inserted using a conventional machine. For accuracy, stitch darts using a conventional machine. Serging darts eliminates any chance of changing the dart position at a later time. Conventional sewing also prevents a dimple or pucker at the point of a dart.

How to Sew Side Seams with Pockets

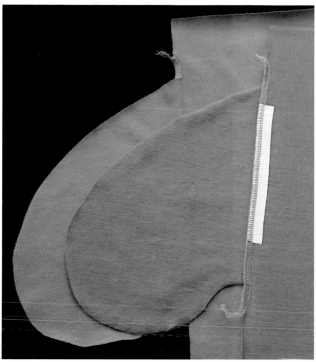

1) Apply ⅜" (1.5 cm) strip of fusible knit interfacing to seam allowance of garment front pocket opening. Serge front pocket to garment front, and back pocket to garment back. Press seams toward pockets.

2) Use conventional machine to stitch garment side seam, with right sides together; stitch from about 3" (7.5 cm) below pocket opening to bottom of pocket opening. Stitch from top of pocket opening to upper edge of garment section.

3) Baste pockets together, using basting glue or glue stick (page 34). (This is especially helpful if pockets are cut from slippery lining fabrics.)

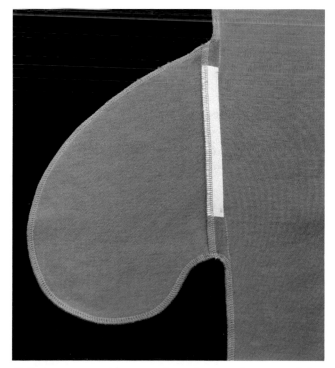

4) Sew garment side seam from lower edge to straight stitching at bottom of pocket opening; then curve stitching around pocket. Continue stitching side seam to waistline. Press pocket and side seam toward front of garment.

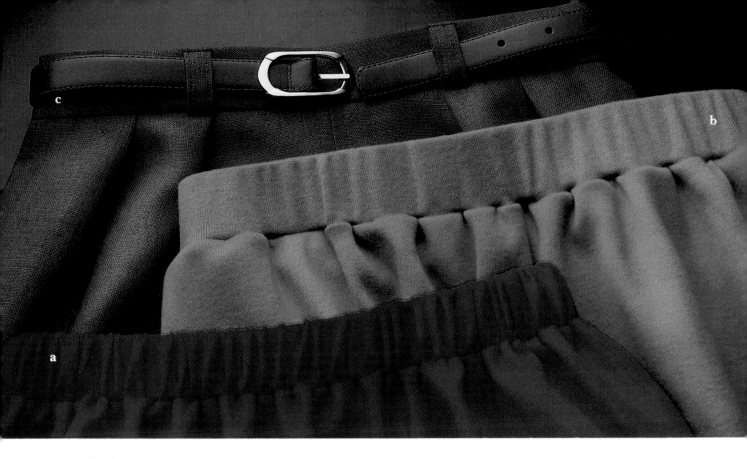

Waistbands

There are several methods for applying waistbands. The cut-on elasticized waistband (a) and the separate elasticized waistband (b) are used for pull-on skirts or pants. The edge-finished waistband (c) is used for skirts or pants with plackets.

A cut-on waistband is a quick waistline finish for either straight-cut skirts or pants. To make a cut-on waistband, extend the pattern above the waistline two times the width of the elastic plus ¾" (2 cm). The upper edge of the garment is folded down to form a casing for the elastic.

The separate elasticized waistband can be cut from self-fabric; or use a lighter-weight fabric, such as ribbing, to eliminate bulk.

The edge-finished waistband uses both the overlock and the conventional machine. To reduce bulk, the inside edge of the waistband is serged, and enclosed seams are sewn conventionally and graded. Attach belt loops at the waistline before applying the waistband.

How to Sew a Cut-on Elasticized Waistband

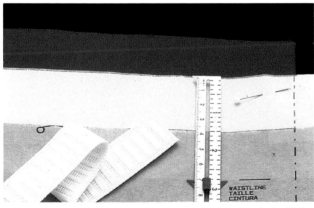

1) **Extend** pattern above waistline two times the width of the elastic plus ¾" (2 cm). For example, for a 1" (2.5 cm) elastic, add 2¾" (7 cm) above the waistline.

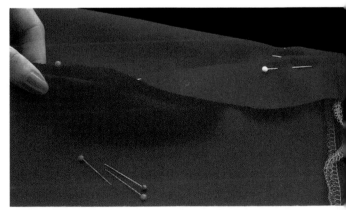

2) **Fold** garment to wrong side the width of the elastic plus ½" (1.3 cm) from raw edge; pin or baste. Fold garment back on itself, with raw edge extending ¼" (6 mm) beyond fold.

How to Apply a Separate Elasticized Waistband

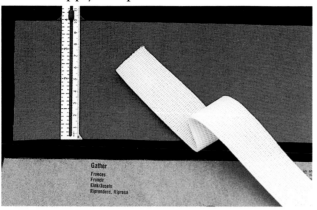

1) Cut waistband two times the width of elastic plus 1½" (3.8 cm) to allow for two ⅝" (1.5 cm) seam allowances plus ¼" (6 mm) ease. If using woven fabric, length of waistband is the same measurement as edge of garment. If using ribbing, length must be long enough to pull over hips.

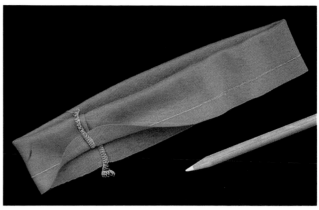

2) Mark seamlines for accurate stitching; this is especially helpful when ribbing is used. Stitch short ends of waistband, right sides together, to form a circle. Fold in half lengthwise.

3) Pin waistband to edge of garment; serge with needle on seamline, leaving 2" (5 cm) opening for inserting elastic. If using ribbing, stretch ribbing to match garment. Remove pins as you come to them.

4) Cut elastic to fit waistline; insert into waistband. Stitch ends of elastic together, using conventional machine. Serge opening closed. Stitch in the ditch at seamline to prevent elastic from twisting, if desired.

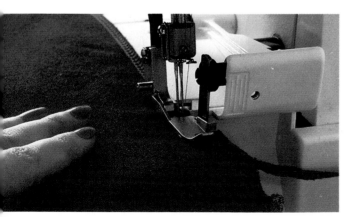

3) Stitch along the fold so stitches catch, but do not cut fold; trim extended seam allowance. Remove pins as you come to them. Leave 2" (5 cm) opening for inserting elastic.

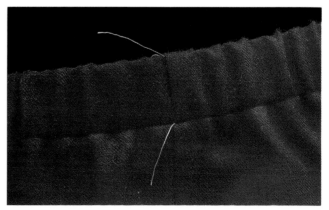

4) Cut elastic to fit waistline; insert into waistband. Stitch ends of elastic together, using conventional machine. Serge opening closed. Stitch in the ditch at seamlines to prevent elastic from twisting, if desired.

How to Apply an Edge-finished Waistband

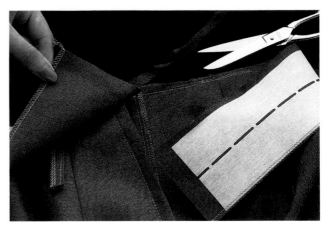

1) Interface waistband. Serge one long side of waistband, trimming ⅜" (1 cm).

2) Baste one end of each belt loop to garment at desired position. Pin waistband to garment, matching pattern markings; straight-stitch, keeping serged edge of waistband free. Grade seam allowance.

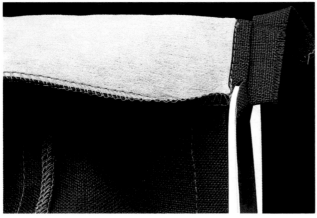

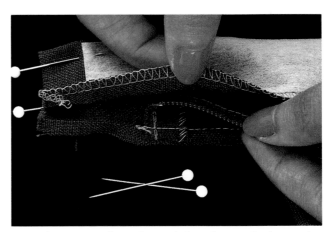

3) Press seam allowances toward waistband. Fold waistband, right sides together. Stitch overlap end of waistband, folding serged seam allowance back to waistline seam; grade.

4) Tuck garment into the waistband at underlap end of garment.

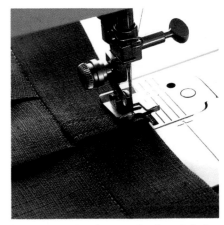

5) Stitch across end and lower edge of underlap; continue stitching over previous stitches through all layers of garment and waistband; stop stitching (arrow) ½" (1.3 cm) beyond underlap dot. Grade.

6) Turn waistband right side out, and press; serged edge extends down on inside of garment. Pin in place. Stitch in the ditch of the seam from right side, using conventional sewing machine.

7) Fold under free end of each belt loop; topstitch to waistband at upper edge.

How to Sew Belt Loops

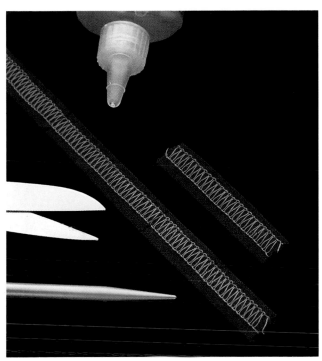

Flatlock belt loops. 1) Cut fabric strip two times the finished width of belt loop; length of strip equals cut length of each belt loop times the number of loops. Fold strip lengthwise, wrong sides together; do not press. Serge long edges together, using flatlock stitch (pages 60 to 63).

2) Insert pencil or knitting needle inside tube to flatten stitches. Center stitches on underside of strip; press. Mark cutting lines. Apply liquid fray preventer at marks; allow to dry. Cut into belt loops.

Topstitched belt loops. 1) Cut strip of fabric three times the finished width of belt loop; length of strip equals cut length of each belt loop times number of loops. Serge one long edge of strip, trimming slightly.

2) Fold strip into thirds lengthwise, enclosing raw edge. Topstitch both edges from right side ⅛" (3 mm) from fold. Mark cutting lines. Apply liquid fray preventer at marks; allow to dry. Cut into belt loops.

Assembling
Skirts & Pants

Once you have learned the overlock methods for sewing pockets, belt loops, and waistbands, assembling skirts or pants is a simple task. Depending on the style of the garment, you may be able to sew the garment completely on the overlock, or use both the overlock and conventional machine.

The skirt shown here uses a combination of conventional and serger methods. The side seams and in-seam pockets are serged, but the center back seam is sewn conventionally so the zipper can be inserted in the seam. Then the pleats are stitched according to the pattern instructions.

Belt loops are serged, and the waistband is applied, using the edge-finished waistband method (page 100), which combines the use of the overlock and the conventional machine. Closures are applied, and the hem is serged and stitched to finish the skirt.

How to Sew a Skirt or Pants Using an Overlock

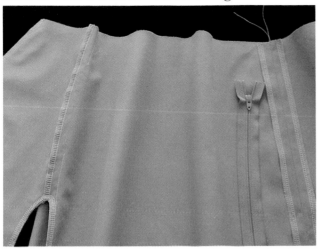

1) Sew seams, stitching in-seam pockets, if included. For seam with zipper opening, use conventional seam with overlocked seam finish. Press seams.

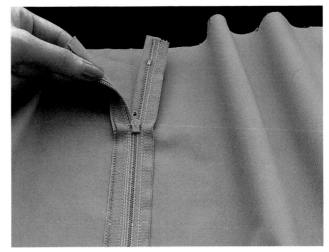

2) Install zipper, using the conventional machine.

3) Stitch darts or pleats according to pattern instructions, or stitch gathered seams (page 71).

4) Make belt loops (page 101). Interface and apply waistband (pages 98 to 100).

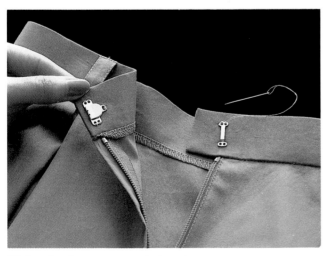

5) Apply closures to waistband.

6) Stitch hem, using desired method (pages 75 to 79). Press garment.

Dresses

The methods used for sewing blouses and skirts are also used for sewing dresses. Refer to pages 89 to 103 for these basic construction methods. Then join the bodice and skirt sections together, using one of several waistline methods.

For dresses with gathered or pleated skirts, use conventional construction methods for the waistline seam and overlock the seam allowances together for a neat, durable finish. Or gather waistline seams, using the overlock method on page 71.

For dresses with elasticized waistline seams, insert the elastic into a casing formed by serging seam allowances together, as shown, opposite.

For dresses without waistline seams, elastic can be added at the waist without the bulk of the usual bias tape casing. Overedge ⅛" (3 mm) oval elastic, as shown, opposite. Leave a side seam or back seam open until after the elastic is applied. This method may be substituted for an elastic casing on gathered or puffed sleeves, especially popular in children's wear.

Some overlock models come with an elastic foot or tape guide that can be used to apply elastic. The techniques for these accessories vary, depending on the model. Refer to the manual for instructions. The instructions for applying elastic on the opposite page do not require the use of any special accessories and can be used for any overlock.

After finishing the waistline seam, you may add belt loops. Chain belt loops can be made quickly using tail chains and have the look of hand-crocheted loops. For sturdier chain loops, use the rolled hem stitch and buttonhole twist or topstitching thread to make the tail chain.

How to Apply Elastic to a Waistline Seam

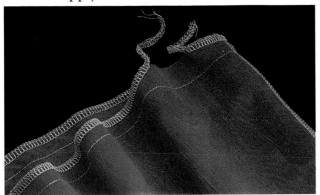

1) Stitch waistline seam, using conventional machine. Serge seam allowances together, trimming slightly; leave 2" (5 cm) opening for inserting elastic.

2) Cut elastic to fit waistline comfortably plus 1" (2.5 cm) for seam allowances. Insert into casing. Using conventional machine, stitch ends of elastic together securely. Serge opening closed.

How to Overedge Elastic at a Placement Line

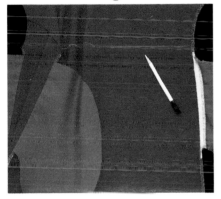

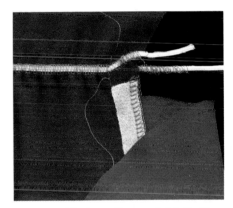

1) Mark placement line for elastic on wrong side of garment pieces. Stitch and press seams, leaving a center back or side seam open. Fold garment on placement line. Adjust machine for flatlock stitch (pages 60 to 63).

2) Position ⅛" (3 mm) elastic under back of presser foot, bringing elastic over foot at front. Stitch along placement line, with elastic between needle and knife; do not stretch elastic or cut fold.

3) Pull fabric to flatten fold. Pull up elastic for a comfortable fit; cut to desired length. Secure ends of elastic using conventional machine. Stitch remaining garment seam. (Ladder of flatlock stitches shows on right side of garment.)

How to Make Chain Belt Loops

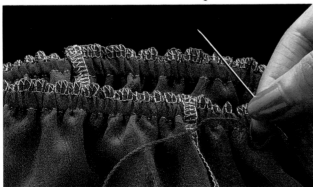

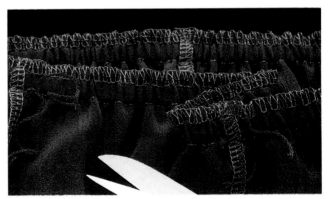

1) Cut a length of rolled hem tail chain for each belt loop three times the length of finished loop. Thread tail chain through large-eyed needle; stitch through garment so ends are on wrong side.

2) Adjust length of loop on right side of garment; pull excess tail chain to wrong side. Tie ends of chain together; clip excess.

Sewing Special Fabrics

Many fabrics require special handling for best results. The weave, pattern, design, and weight of the fabric all affect the finished seams. To anticipate problems, always test-sew on fabric scraps across both grainlines and on the bias before constructing a garment.

Some overlocks have a differential-feed system, which can be used to prevent puckered or stretched seams on special fabrics. The differential feed automatically stretches, eases, or gathers the fabric when the amount of feed of the front feed dog is changed in relation to that of the rear feed dog. This feature is especially helpful when sewing lightweight fabrics that pucker, such as sheers, or fabrics that stretch out of shape easily, such as sweater knits and fabrics cut on the bias.

The factory-set pressure on the presser foot is suitable for most fabrics, but for some lightweight or heavyweight fabrics, it may be helpful to adjust the pressure, opposite.

Sheers (1) and **silkies (2)** require a new needle (size 70/10 or 75/11) and a shorter stitch length (1.5 to 2 mm). Use taut sewing, below, or differential feed, opposite, when stitching these lightweight fabrics to prevent puckered seams. If necessary, the needle thread tension may also be loosened slightly to prevent puckering, but this may cause needle thread to show on the right side of the garment.

Laces (3) require a short stitch length (2 mm) and a narrow stitch width (2.5 to 3.5 mm). Use taut sewing or differential feed to prevent puckering. Uneven stitching cannot be avoided because of thick and thin areas on lace. Open-weave laces may not have enough surface on which the overlock can stitch. A strip of

tricot bias binding can be sewn into the seam to give a complete surface for the overlock to stitch.

Fabrics with raised designs (4), such as matelassé and eyelet, may also cause irregular stitches due to the uneven texture. For this reason, do not use decorative stitching on these fabrics. Plan for seamlines to fall between eyelet embroideries, if possible; and if using a rolled hem finish on eyelet, plan for the stitches to fall between the eyelet designs.

Sweater knit fabrics (5) require special handling to prevent stretched seams. Use the differential feed if your overlock has this feature, or ease the fabric into the machine. For more information on sewing sweater knits, see pages 108 and 109.

Quilted fabrics (6) may be too thick to feed into the knives, restricting the trimming function of the machine. Compress the thick layers with a row of straight or zigzag stitches, using a conventional machine. Sew, allowing the knives to cut on this stitching line.

Decorator fabrics (7) can be serged easily. For easier stitching of large pieces, such as drapery panels, do not allow the fabric to hang over the edge of the table. Trim away selvages as you stitch drapery seams, to avoid puckering.

Fake fur (8) can be seamed with the flatlock stitch (pages 60 to 63) to eliminate bulky and twisted seams. Completely trim away the seam allowances before sewing, and place the fur right sides together, pushing fur fibers away from the seamline. Then flatlock the seam without trimming, and pull the seam flat.

Preventing Puckered or Stretched Seams

Taut sewing. Hold fabric firmly in front of and behind the presser foot while stitching, to prevent puckered seams. Do not pull fabric through the machine. Sew at an even speed for smooth stitching.

Easing fabric. Hold fabric loosely in front of the presser foot, allowing the machine to feed it readily, to prevent stretched seams. Do not hold fabric behind the presser foot.

Adjusting differential feed. Adjust the differential-feed feature, if available on your overlock, to prevent puckered or stretched seams. The setting will differ, depending on the fabric. Stitch without taut sewing or easing fabric, allowing machine to feed fabric automatically.

Adjusting presser foot pressure. Adjust the pressure, if necessary. For lightweight fabrics, turn the pressure-regulating screw to the left; for heavyweight fabrics, turn it to the right. This adjustment may be helpful if it is inconvenient to guide fabric using taut sewing or easing fabric.

Sweaters

Sweater fabrics are available in several forms. Sweater-bodies, panels with prefinished ribbed edges, are available with ribbing to match. Sweater knit yardage can be purchased on the bolt with ribbing yardage to match; or knit your own sweater yardage or panels using a knitting machine or by hand.

Cut sweater knit fabric allowing 1" (2.5 cm) seam allowances, except for ribbing seams. The overlock handles the fabric better, without stretching it, when a larger seam allowance is trimmed. Cut and fit ribbing for necklines or cuffs, as directed below, allowing ¼" (6 mm) seam allowances.

Sweater knit fabric may stretch out of shape when sewn. To prevent seams from stretching, use the differential feed if your machine has this feature, or ease the fabric under the presser foot as you stitch (pages 106 and 107). To sew sweater knits, 3-thread overlock or 4/3-thread mock safety stitches may be used, but they may not recover well when stretched. You may prefer the 4-thread or 5-thread safety stitches, which are more stable.

How to Cut a Sweater Body

1) Lay sweater body on cutting surface that can be pinned into. Stretch ribbed edge to same size as body of panel; pin to cutting surface.

2) Fold up hem allowance on pattern, if included. Lay pattern on fabric with fold at ribbed edge. Cut, allowing 1" (2.5 cm) seam allowances.

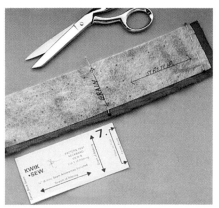

3) Cut neckline ribbing, using the pattern guide. Check fit of ribbing around neck, opposite.

How to Cut Ribbing

Straight edges. Fold ribbing in half lengthwise; pin-fit around body. Ribbing should lie flat without gaping. Do not distort ribs. Add ½" (1.3 cm) for seam allowances.

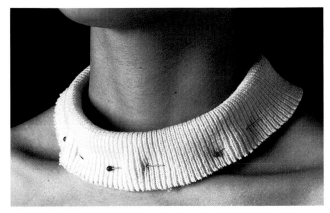

Necklines. Cut ribbing according to pattern guide. Stitch ribbing seam, and fold in half lengthwise. Check fit around neck; adjust ribbing seam if necessary.

Tips for Sweater Knit Seams

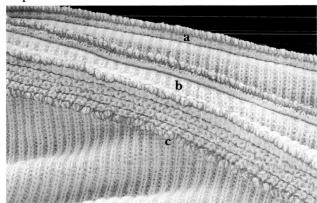

Stabilize shoulder seams with transparent elastic (**a**) or tricot bias binding (**b**), as on page 73. Or use a conventional seam with serged seam finishes, and edgestitch seam on each side (**c**).

Sew sleeves to garment with the sleeve cap facing down, easing the sleeve into the armhole; do not stretch the armhole.

How to Apply Ribbing to a Sweater

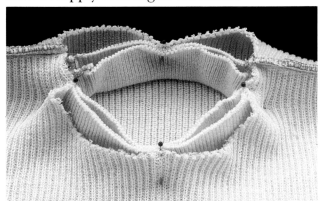

1) Stitch ends of ribbing, right sides together; fold in half lengthwise. Divide ribbing and garment edges into fourths; mark. Pin ribbing to garment, right sides together, matching markings.

2) Stitch with ribbing on top. Ease garment edge to match ribbing; do not stretch garment or ribbing.

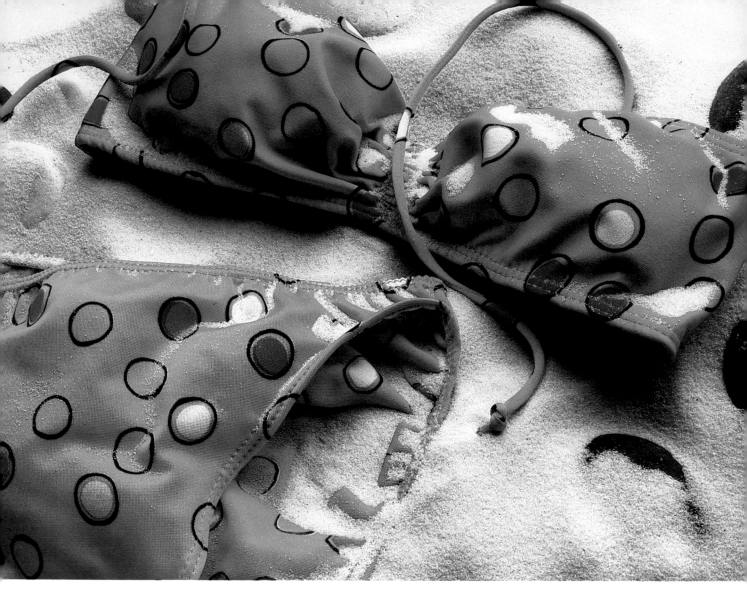

Swimwear

Overlocks or sergers that have stretch stitches are perfect for sewing swimwear. A 3-thread or 4-thread mock safety stitch, or a 3-thread overlock stitch is recommended for strong, stretchy seams. These seams stretch with two-way stretch fabrics, allowing for comfort and unrestricted action.

Test the stitch tension adjustment on a fabric scrap before sewing the garment, stitching on both crosswise and lengthwise grains. After adjusting the tensions so the looper threads lock at the edge, check for correct needle thread tension by stretching the fabric. If the needle threads break, loosen the needle thread tension. Needle threads should be just loose enough to prevent thread breakage when seams are stretched, and as tight as necessary to prevent threads from showing noticeably on the right side of the garment.

Because of the close fit of swimsuits, seams have a tendency to pull open and expose the needle threads, even when tensions are adjusted. Thread that closely matches the fabric makes this less noticeable. Woolly

nylon thread in the needle is also helpful; it tightens up the stitches yet stretches with the fabric. Woolly nylon can also be used in the loopers for seams that are soft, comfortable, and strong; this is important for close-fitting garments.

Use transparent elastic or chlorine-resistant elastic for sewing swimwear. Transparent elastic is lighter in weight than chlorine-resistant elastic, for a smoother fit. There is also less concern about cutting into transparent elastic with the knives, because it does not fray when trimmed.

The in-the-round method of construction is recommended for smooth, strong elasticized edges. Elastic is easier to apply in the round than with the flat method, because you can stretch the elastic in front of and behind the presser foot at all times. When the flat method is used, it is more difficult to start stitching on the elastic unless a few extra inches (2.5 cm) of elastic are extended behind the presser foot at the beginning of the seam.

How to Apply Elastic in the Round

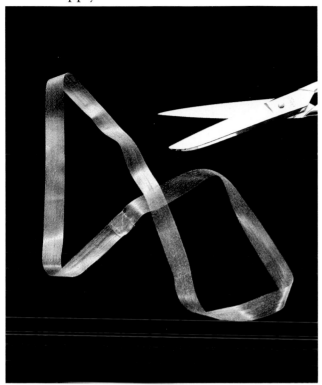

1) **Measure** and cut elastic. Lap ends ½" (1.3 cm); stitch on conventional machine.

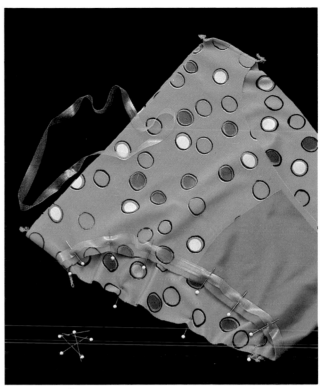

2) **Pin** elastic to garment, *wrong* sides together, matching pattern markings. Place inside edge of elastic on seamline.

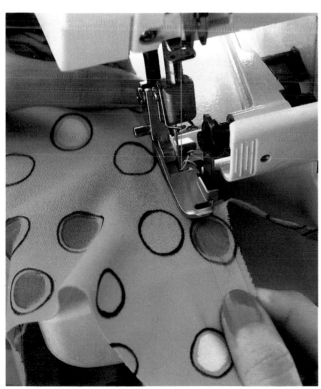

3) **Stitch,** using long stitches (5 mm); trim ¼" (6 mm) if pattern has ⅝" (1.5 cm) seam allowances. Do not cut elastic with knives.

4) **Fold** elastic to inside of garment. Use long stitches, and loosen the tension on conventional machine; topstitch from the right side of garment with a twin needle, using woolly nylon thread in the bobbin.

Special Effects

Decorative Ideas for the Home

Overlocks or sergers are great time-savers when you are sewing for the home. Trim selvages from long drapery seams as you stitch, or neatly finish gathered seams and rolled hems on ruffled curtains. Then add the finishing touches to a decorating project with the use of decorative stitches.

Pillows. Add decorative touches, such as pin tucks, lace, or ribbon. Sew these details according to the directions, opposite.

Ruffled curtains. Use fine monofilament nylon thread for a nearly invisible rolled hem finish on single-layer ruffles, or stitch rolled hems using contrasting decorative thread for an accent. Differential feed makes gathering ruffles faster and easier.

Placemats and napkins. Use woolly nylon for decorative edge finishes, loosening looper tensions to achieve a lofty, filled-in edge.

How to Apply Lace and Ribbon

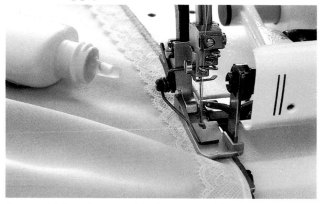

Lace. Fold and press fabric, *wrong* sides together, on placement line. Place lace on top of fabric, right side up, so straight edge of lace is aligned with fold; glue-baste. Flatlock on the fold (page 72). Lace edging is caught in stitches.

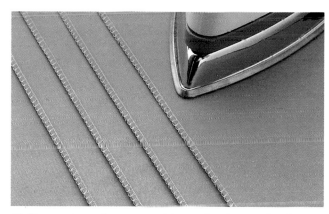

Lace and ribbon. Fold fabric, and glue-baste lace, as shown, left. Place ⅛" (3 mm) ribbon under back of presser foot and over front of presser foot. Place fabric and lace under ribbon. Flatlock on the fold (page 72); hold ribbon to the right of needle as you stitch over it; do not catch ribbon in stitches.

How to Sew Pin Tucks

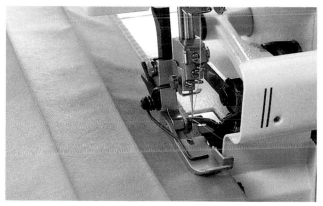

1) Fold and press fabric, *wrong* sides together, on placement line. Raise upper knife into disengaged position. Stitch, using balanced 3-thread overlock tension (pages 55 to 57), so fold of fabric is aligned with edge of needle plate.

2) Press pin tucks to one side so the decorative loops are visible.

How to Gather Fabric Using Differential Feed

1) Adjust differential feed for gathering. Weight of fabric affects fullness of gathers. (Not all models have differential feed.)

2) Gather fabric by serging along edge; test-sew on fabric scrap before stitching project. Machine gathers fabric automatically.

Ideas for Decorative Stitching

Decorative threads can be used in many ways to add a special effect to your projects. Some ideas are shown here, and after learning how to use decorative threads in your overlock (pages 118 to 123), you can create ideas of your own.

Stitch around simple shapes, such as circles, triangles, and squares, for an appliqué effect. Fuse or glue-baste in place. Topstitch through overlock stitches to secure.

Eliminate facings on a jacket made of fabrics such as boiled wool. Stitch outer edges, using yarn or other decorative threads. Use wrapped overedge stitch (page 119) for a reversible effect on lapel.

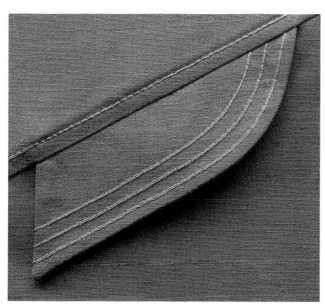

Use chainstitch (pages 55 and 58) as decorative topstitching. Stitch with right side of garment facing down.

Flatlock several rows of stitching (page 72). Sew rows of flatlocking parallel to a design line, such as this raglan seam, or create your own random design lines.

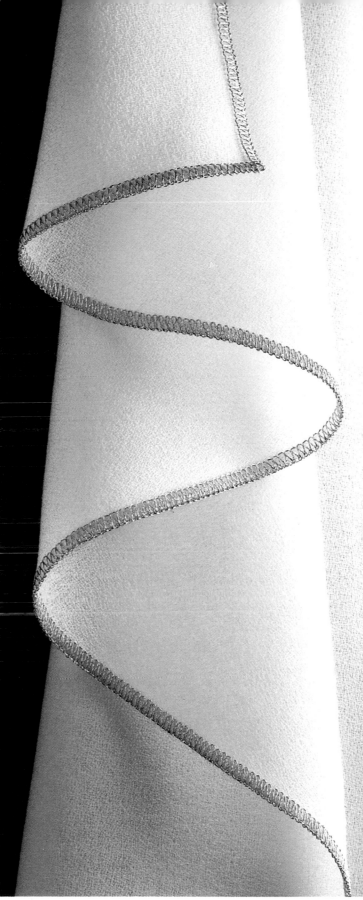

Use two colors of thread for a special effect on garment edges. Use balanced 3-thread overlock stitch (pages 55 to 57), and use two decorative threads in upper and lower loopers (page 119).

117

Special Decorative Stitches

With the use of decorative threads, an overlock or serger can duplicate the look of fine braids and bindings previously found only in ready-to-wear. Decorative threads for use in an overlock can be found in fabric, craft, needlework, and yarn stores, as well as through sewing machine dealers.

The finished effect of the decorative thread will depend on the width and length of the stitch as well as on the thread being used. When using decorative techniques, it is necessary to test-sew each thread and fabric to determine how to achieve the desired result. Practice sewing with a variety of stitch length, width, and tension adjustments.

If a decorative thread is lightweight, strong, and does not fray, it can be used in the needle and both loopers.

When decorative thread is used only in a looper, it is laid on the fabric surface, because the looper threads do not penetrate the fabric. Usually, decorative thread is only used for the looper thread that forms the most noticeable part of the stitch, and regular sewing thread or fine monofilament nylon thread is used in the other looper and the needle.

It is often easier to use decorative thread in the upper looper than in the lower looper, because there are fewer thread guides for the decorative thread to follow. Some threads may fray or break when used in the lower looper. For this reason, if you have a choice between using 2-thread or 3-thread flatlock stitches on your serger, you may prefer 3-thread flatlocking when using heavier decorative threads.

Decorative 3-thread Stitches

Use decorative thread in the upper looper for 3-thread flatlock stitch (shown) or 3-thread rolled hem stitch, because upper looper thread forms the decorative loops of these stitches.

Decorative 2-thread Stitches

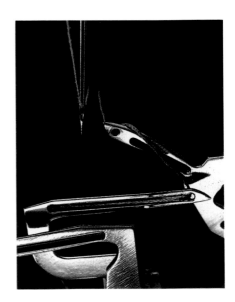

Use decorative thread in the looper for 2-thread flatlock stitch (shown), or 3-thread rolled hem stitch, because the looper thread forms the decorative loops of these stitches. (Upper and chainstitch loopers are unthreaded when using a 5-thread overlock.)

3-thread or 2-thread Decorative Edges

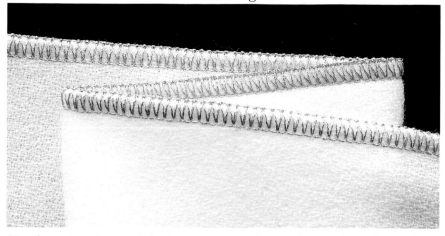

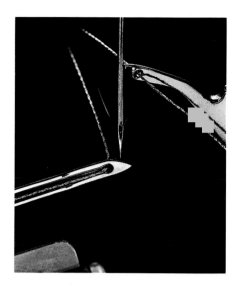

Use decorative thread in both the upper and lower loopers for a decorative edge on both sides of the fabric.

3-thread Wrapped Overedge Stitches

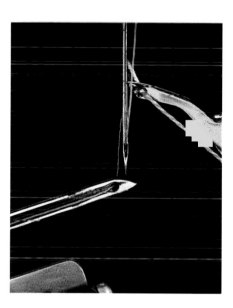

Use decorative thread in the upper looper. Loosen upper looper thread tension dial so thread wraps completely around the edge; tighten lower looper thread tension dial until lower looper thread forms a straight line.

2-thread Wrapped Overedge Stitches

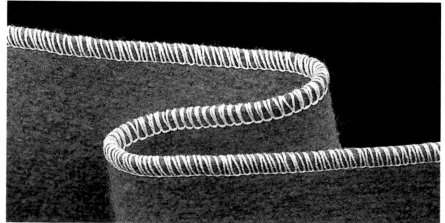

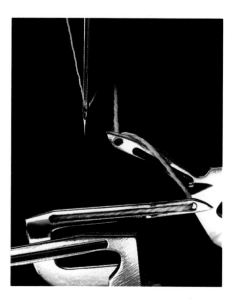

Use decorative thread in the lower looper. Loosen looper thread tension dial so looper thread wraps completely around the edge; tighten needle thread tension dial to hold stitches taut. (Upper and chainstitch loopers are unthreaded when using a 5-thread overlock.)

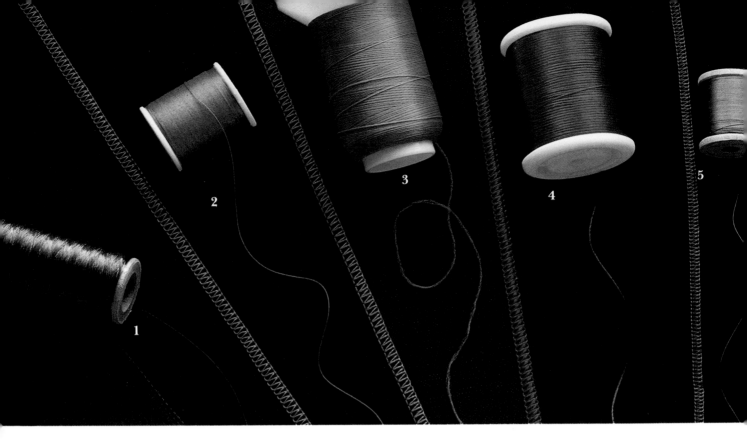

Selecting Decorative Threads

Not all decorative threads will work in all overlocks. You will need to do some testing (pages 122 to 123) to find out which threads will be most successful for you. Do not assume that, because a certain thread works in your friend's machine, it will also work in yours. Even overlocks of the same model and brand may handle threads differently. If your machine does not handle a certain thread well, you may be able to find a substitute that gives a similar effect.

When experimenting with decorative threads in the overlock, start with lightweight and smooth-textured threads, which require fewer tension adjustments. Avoid quilting thread; although it is lightweight, it is too stiff to feed easily through the machine.

The amount of decorative thread required varies, depending on the size of the thread, the stitch length and width, and the total length of decorative stitching on the project. Measure the distance to be sewn with decorative stitching; add one extra yard (.95 m) to this length for test-sewing. For each looper, allow 9 to 10 yards (8.25 to 9.15 m) of decorative thread per yard (.95 m) of decorative stitching. A lightweight thread requires more yardage for complete coverage than a heavyweight thread.

Monofilament nylon, topstitching thread, and woolly nylon are the easiest decorative threads to use in an overlock. They require minor tension adjustments and can be used in both loopers, and in the needles.

Fine monofilament nylon (1) can be used to blend stitches with the fabric, such as for rolled hems on multicolored fabrics. Or use it in the needle and lower looper when sewing a 3-thread overlock stitch, with a heavy decorative thread in the upper looper; the nylon thread blends into the decorative loops.

Topstitching thread (2) or buttonhole twist can be used in loopers and needles, but is most often used in loopers only, with regular or monofilament thread in the needles. Use topstitching thread or buttonhole twist in the upper and lower looper to sew a balanced 3-thread overlock stitch that is decorative, although not identical, on both sides of the fabric.

Woolly nylon thread (3) is easy to use on the overlock or serger, although it has a fuzzy appearance. Woolly nylon is soft, comfortable, and strong, and is ideal for activewear and swimwear. Woolly nylon adds tension, making it perfect for use in the lower looper when sewing a 3-thread rolled hem or 3-thread flatlock stitch. Tension can be loosened on woolly nylon thread for a lofty, filled-in edge finish.

Rayon, silk, and metallic threads require more tension adjustment, but are not difficult to use. They are easier to use in the upper looper than in the lower looper.

Rayon (4) and silk (5) threads are available in several weights. Because the threads are very smooth, use nets to prevent them from spilling off the spool and to control them with a little extra tension on the

6   7   8   9   10

spool. Also, tighten the tension dial to prevent them from slipping between the tension discs.

Metallic thread (6) is available in gold, silver, and colors. Some metallics will fray if used in the lower looper. There are several different types of metallic thread, some more fragile than others. For easier serging, select filament threads, which do not fray or strip easily from the core.

Crochet thread, pearl cotton, ribbon, and yarn are the heaviest or thickest decorative threads and require a greater amount of tension adjustment. They may not feed well through the lower looper. It may be necessary to loosen the tension dial as much as possible. To ensure even feeding of balls or skeins, feed the thread by hand, making sure there is always slack in the thread as it enters the first thread guide (page 123).

Crochet thread (7) is available in cotton or acrylic and comes wound in balls. It is tightly twisted and can be used in both loopers.

Pearl cotton (8) also comes wound in balls and is available in two weights, #8 and #5. The #8 thread is finer and easier to use. Pearl cotton is less twisted than crochet cotton. It works well in the upper looper, but may fray if used in the lower looper.

Ribbon (9) up to ¼" (6 mm) wide can be used if it is lightweight, soft, and pliable, such as ribbons designed for knitting. You may find knitting ribbon

on cones, spools, or cards. It is available in acrylic, cotton, rayon, and silk. Polyester ribbon is usually not pliable enough to be used in the looper, but can be laid flat and overedged with a serged stitch (page 115) for a decorative effect.

Yarn (10) must be smooth and tightly twisted to feed evenly through the machine. It also must be fine enough to thread through the eye of the upper looper easily and strong enough to feed through the thread guides. Yarn tends to stretch as it is sewn, so you may need to loosen the tension completely.

Tips for Selecting Decorative Threads

Select thread with a smooth, tight twist. Thread that is spun unevenly or that has a nubby texture does not feed smoothly.

Select thread that is strong. Thread that frays or has weak, thin areas will break easily.

Select soft, flexible threads that slide smoothly through the thread guides and the eye of the looper. Thread that is stiff or nonpliable does not feed smoothly.

Select thread that can be threaded through the eye of the looper without resistance. Thread that is too heavy or thick can break the looper or disturb the timing of the machine.

Select thread of an appropriate weight for the fabric. Thread that is too heavy causes puckering.

Select thread that has the same care method as the fabric.

Adjusting the Decorative Stitch

The stitch width and stitch length control not only how wide or how far apart the stitches will be, but also the final appearance of the decorative stitching.

For stitch length, the general rule of adjustment is: the finer the thread, the shorter the stitch length. Short stitches are used for fine, lightweight threads (1 to 2 mm) to make the stitching more noticeable. Heavier threads require a longer stitch length (4 to 5 mm) to allow for the thickness of the thread, so it can lay in even curves on the fabric. Heavy threads do not curve and bend as easily with short stitches. When stitches are too close together, the loops of heavy thread may pile up, causing a fabric jam.

Varying the stitch width also changes the appearance of the stitching. Stitch width is mostly a matter of personal preference, but, generally, a narrower stitch is used with fine, lightweight threads; a wider stitch, with heavy threads.

How to Test-sew Decorative Thread

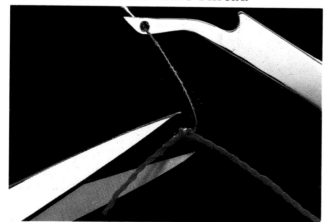

1) Thread serger, tying on threads (pages 30 and 31); do not pull the knots through loopers when using heavy thread.

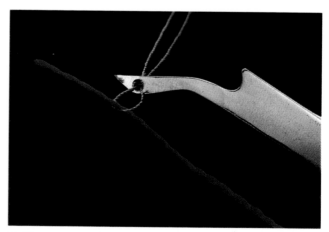

2) Use strand of all-purpose thread to form a loop; thread through eye of looper. Place the decorative thread through the loop, and pull through the eye.

3) Use a net on thread if thread tends to slide or spill off the spool or for any thread that feeds unevenly.

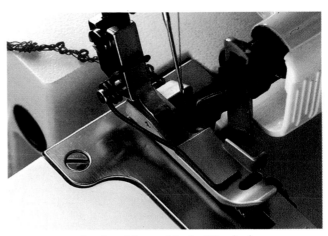

4) Test-sew slowly without fabric. Watch the area around stitch fingers to see if stitches are forming.

5) Loosen tension if thread does not feed through serger. It may be necessary to loosen tension completely or skip a thread guide if it pinches the thread. (On some sergers, you may need to bypass tension disc.)

6) Lift presser foot, and place fabric scrap under foot; stitch slowly, checking stitch formation on fabric. Adjust tension, stitch length, and stitch width, until desired stitch is achieved.

Tips for Even Feeding of Decorative Thread

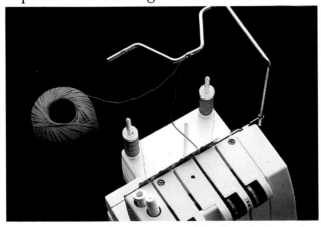

Feed thread into first thread guide directly from the ball, skein, or card, if thread is not wound on a spool. Reel thread off ball by hand. Keep decorative thread slack in the area of thread guide holder to prevent uneven stitches. It is especially important to watch for this if using thread directly from a ball.

Place cardboard shim under presser foot before and after an intersecting seam, so stitch length remains even at thick seam allowances; position shim so needle does not stitch through it.

Troubleshooting Chart

Problem	Possible Solutions	Page Reference
Fabric puckers	**Check** threading.	pages 30 and 31
	Check for tangled or caught thread.	pages 30 and 31
	Use high-quality lightweight thread.	page 22
	Shorten stitch length.	pages 53 and 54
	Loosen thread tension.	pages 55 to 67
	Use differential-feed feature, if available.	pages 108 and 109
	Hold fabric taut in front of and behind presser foot while sewing.	page 108
	Decrease presser foot pressure for lightweight fabric.	pages 108 and 109
	Check alignment and sharpness of knives.	page 27
Fabric stretches	**Trim** ¼" (6 mm) or more while sewing; for sweater knits, trim ¾" (2 cm), except when applying ribbing.	pages 108 and 114
	Lengthen stitch length.	pages 52 and 53
	Use differential-feed feature, if available.	pages 108 and 109
	Ease fabric into overlock while sewing; do not stretch fabric.	page 108
	Stabilize seam.	pages 69 and 73
	Decrease presser foot pressure for lightweight or stretchy fabric.	pages 108 and 109
Fabric jams	**Close** looper cover before sewing.	page 12
	Do not allow trimmings to fall into machine.	page 46
	Check for tangled or caught thread.	pages 30 and 31
	Compress thick layers of fabric with conventional stitches before serging.	page 46
	Lengthen stitch length.	pages 52 and 53
	Loosen looper thread tensions.	pages 55 to 67
	Check alignment and sharpness of knives.	page 27
Fabric does not feed well	**Lower** presser foot.	page 36
	Lengthen stitch length.	pages 52 and 53
	Use differential-feed feature, if available.	pages 108 and 109
	Increase presser foot pressure for heavyweight fabric.	pages 108 and 109
	Decrease presser foot pressure for lightweight fabric.	pages 108 and 109
	Check alignment and sharpness of knives.	page 27
Fabric layers shift at beginning of seam	**Lift** presser foot and position fabric under it.	page 36
	Glue-baste between layers of fabric.	page 34
Fabric trims unevenly	**Trim** at least slightly while stitching.	page 33
	Use tricot bias binding to eliminate ragged edges on rolled hems.	page 79
	Check alignment and sharpness of knives.	page 27

Problem	Possible Solutions	Page Reference
Stitches skip	**Check** threading.	pages 30 and 31
	Use high-quality thread.	page 22
	Change type of thread.	page 22
	Insert needle correctly.	page 27
	Tighten needle set screw.	page 27
	Change a dull, damaged, or defective needle to a new needle.	page 27
	Change type or size of needle.	page 27
	Loosen thread tension.	pages 55 to 67
	Do not stitch through heavy application of water-soluble glue stick.	page 34
	Allow overlock to feed fabric, or hold fabric taut in front of and behind presser foot while sewing.	page 108
	Do not pull fabric through machine from behind presser foot.	page 108
	Increase presser foot pressure for heavyweight fabric.	pages 108 and 109
Stitches are irregular	**Check** threading.	pages 30 and 31
	Thread must feed from spool smoothly.	pages 30, 31, and 122
	Use high-quality, evenly twisted thread.	pages 22, 120, and 121
	Adjust thread tension.	pages 55 to 67, 120 to 121, 123
	Insert needle correctly.	page 27
	Change a dull, damaged, or defective needle to a new needle.	page 27
	Change type or size of needle.	page 27
	Use fabric that has an even texture for decorative stitching.	page 108
	Check alignment and sharpness of knives.	page 27
Needle breaks	**Check** for tangled or caught thread.	pages 30 and 31
	Insert needle correctly.	page 27
	Tighten needle set screw.	page 27
	Change to larger-size needle.	page 27
	Do not pull fabric through machine from behind presser foot.	page 108
Thread breaks	**Check** threading.	pages 30 and 31
	Check for tangled or caught thread.	pages 30 and 31
	Use high-quality, strong thread.	pages 22, 120, and 121
	Loosen thread tension.	pages 55 to 67, 120 to 121, 123
	Insert needle correctly.	page 27
	Change a dull, damaged, or defective needle to a new needle.	page 27

Index

Cy DeCosse Incorporated offers
sewing accessories to subscribers.
For information write:

Sewing Accessories
5900 Green Oak Drive
Minnetonka, MN 55343